COUNSELLING AND PSYCHOTHERAPY WITH CHILDREN AND ADOLESCENTS

BASIC TEXT IN COUNSELLING AND PSYCHOTHERAPY

Series Editor: Stephen Frosh

This series introduces readers to the theory and practice of counselling and psychotherapy across a wide range of topic areas. The books will appeal to anyone wishing to use counselling and psychotherapeutic skills and are particularly relevant to workers in health, education, social work and related settings. The books in this series are unusual in being rooted in psychodynamic and systemic ideas, yet being written at an accessible, readable and introductory level. Each text offers theoretical background and guidance for practice, with creative use of clinical examples.

Published

Jenny Altschuler
WORKING WITH CHRONIC ILLNESS

Bill Barnes, Sheila Ernst and Keith Hyde
AN INTRODUCTION TO GROUPWORK

Stephen Briggs
WORKING WITH ADOLESCENTS

Alex Coren
SHORT-TERM PSYCHOTHERAPY

Emilia Dowling and Gill Gorell Barnes
WORKING WITH CHILDREN AND PARENTS THROUGH SEPARATION AND DIVORCE

Loretta Franklin
AN INTRODUCTION TO WORKPLACE COUNSELLING

Gill Gorell Barnes
FAMILY THERAPY IN CHANGING TIMES 2nd ed.

Fran Hedges
AN INTRODUCTION TO SYSTEMIC THERAPY WITH INDIVIDUALS

Sally Hodges
COUNSELLING ADULTS WITH LEARNING DISABILITIES

Ravi Rana
COUNSELLING STUDENTS

Tricia Scott
INTEGRATIVE PSYCHOTHERAPY IN HEALTH CARE

Geraldine Shipton
WORKING WITH EATING DISORDERS

Laurence Spurling
AN INTRODUCTION TO PSYCHODYNAMIC COUNSELLING

Paul Terry
COUNSELLING THE ELDERLY AND THEIR CARERS

Steven Walker
CULTURALLY COMPETENT THERAPY

Jan Wiener and Mannie Sher
COUNSELLING AND PSYCHOTHERAPY IN PRIMARY HEALTH CARE

Shula Wilson
DISABILITY, COUNSELLING AND PSYCHOTHERAPY

Invitation to authors

The Series Editor welcomes proposals for new books within the Basic Texts in Counselling and Psychotherapy series. These should be sent to Stephen Frosh at the School of Psychology, Birkbeck College, Malet Street, London WCIE 7HX (email s.frosh@bbk.ac.uk).

Basic Texts in Counselling and Psychotherapy
Series Standing Order ISBN 0–333–69330–2
(*outside North America only*)

You can receive future titles in this series as they are published by placing a standing order. Please contact your bookseller or, in the case of difficulty, write to us at the address below with your name and address, the title of the series and the ISBN quoted above.

Customer Services Department, Macmillan Distribution Ltd.
Houndmills, Basingstoke, Hampshire RG21 6XS, England

COUNSELLING AND PSYCHOTHERAPY WITH CHILDREN AND ADOLESCENTS

LINDA HOPPER

First Published 2007 by
PALGRAVE MACMILLAN
Houndmills, Basingstoke, Hampshire RG21 6XS and
175 Fifth Avenue, New York, N.Y. 10010
Companies and representatives throughout the world

PALGRAVE MACMILLAN is the global academic imprint of the Palgrave
Macmillan division of St. Martin's Press, LLC and of Palgrave Macmillan Ltd.
Macmillan® is a registered trademark in the United States, United Kingdom
and other countries. Palgrave is a registered trademark in the European
Union and other countries.

ISBN–13: 978 1–4039–9791–3 paperback
ISBN–10: 1–4039–9791–8 paperback

This book is printed on paper suitable for recycling and made from fully
managed and sustained forest sources.

A catalogue record for this book is available from the British Library.

A catalog record for this book is available from the Library of Congress.

10 9 8 7 6 5 4 3 2 1
16 15 14 13 12 11 10 09 08 07

Printed in China

To my seven grandchildren
Haidee, Thorney, Orson, Edward, Nushmia, Elana and Christian,
who are so special

CONTENTS

PREFACE

Attending a seminar led by Barbara Dockar-Drysdale in 1981 was the beginning of my therapeutic experience. I was to meet her again in 1990 when she launched the new MA in Therapeutic Child Care course at the University of Reading. She was an inspirational speaker and writer and her work with emotionally distressed children was remarkable.

Having trained as a counsellor with the addition of the Therapeutic Child Care training, I found a great need in Essex for a local counselling service and was the founding Director of the Sycamore counselling and training centre. On relocating to Scotland, I found a lack of training and services in children's counselling. Having run a Diploma programme in Essex, training five cohorts of students, this book draws on material from the course. Training is very much an experiential environment and the practical and clinical work enhance the theoretical components. In written form, this dimension is not available, but I hope that the reader will find the book helpful.

There are some excellent child psychotherapy courses available. The problem is that those who would engage in such training have to invest an inordinate amount of time and money to pursue it, and for most people this is out of the question. The other problem is that usually psychotherapy is practised three times a week or more. This makes the service out of the reach of most families seeking help. But this does not mean that nothing can be done.

One of the most remarkable features of counselling children is that there are many people who are trained to work with adults who are assuming that they can transfer their skills to working with children. In other fields, there is an expectation that people will train for the fields in which they will work. The British Association for Counselling and Psychotherapy (BACP) makes it clear that counsellors should only work within their area of training and expertise. There are also supervisors who are taking on child counsellors as supervisees, who have not worked with children themselves, nor are aware of the differences. Some supervisors offer to do this work in order to learn more about the work with children themselves. This then starts to exploit the work for the benefit of the supervisor and does not give the child client the best service. Unless training has been given, neither the counsellor nor supervisor can claim that they are selecting the best therapeutic interventions.

There are some very special differences in working with children. Counsellors entering this field should not use children to develop their skills. They should have training before seeing child clients and be sure of receiving supervision from those who have experience of working with children. The need for training is being recognized more than before, but it is still not sufficiently available to cope with demand.

I have chosen, for ease of writing, to assign the feminine gender to the counsellor and the masculine to the client. The reverse can be equally acceptable, and maybe the reason for choosing the former is simply that I have practised as a counsellor for many years and happen to be female. The examples retain the gender of the child and therapist.

The words 'counsellor' and 'therapist' are used interchangeably in the text. I have avoided using the word 'psychotherapist' in deference to those who have undergone long years of training and analysis and whose work is usually more intense in the number of times per week the client is seen.

Confidentiality has been maintained by combining and changing the circumstances of some clients. Every example comes from a genuine case or number of cases, but has been rewritten in a way that protects any client from being recognizable.

ACKNOWLEDGEMENTS

Permission has been kindly given for the following quotations, for which we are grateful:

Crown Copyright for quotation from *www.teachernet.gov.uk/wholeschool/sen/ypmentalhealth/factsand__figs/* © Crown Copyright.

Paterson Mark Ltd for quotations from D. Winnicott, *The Child, the Family and the Outside World*, Pelican Books, 1964; Brunner-Routledge for quotations from M. Lanyado, *The Presence of the Therapist*, Brunner-Routledge, 2004; D. Winnicott, *Playing and Reality*, Tavistock, 1971; M. Hunter, *Psychotherapy with Young People in Care: Lost and Found*, Brunner-Routledge, 2001; M. Lanyado & A. Horne (eds), *The Handbook of Child and Adolescent Psychotherapy*, Routledge, 2000; C. Clulow (ed.), *Adult Attachment and Couple Psychotherapy: The 'Secure Base' in Practice and Research*, Brunner-Routledge, 2001; and S. Jennings et al., *The Handbook of Dramatherapy*, Routledge, 1995.

Cathy Miller Rights Agency for quotations from B. Dockar-Drysdale, *Therapy and Consultation in Child Care*, Free Association Books, 1993; and B. Dockar-Drysdale, *The Provision of Primary Experience: Winnicottian Work with Children and Adolescents*, Free Association Books, 1990.

Palgrave Macmillan for quotations from L. Spurling, *An Introduction to Psychodynamic Counselling*, Palgrave Macmillan, 2004.

Westminster John Knox Press for quotations reproduced from *The Angry Christian*, © 2003 Andrew D. Lester.

I wish to express my gratitude to all those who have shaped this book – my colleagues at Sycamore, particularly Eunice Stagg and Barbara Bland, whose support I greatly valued, and the many clients, whose stories have expanded my therapeutic experience and strengthened my practice. My particular thanks to Neville Singh, who read the manuscripts and commented most helpfully and sent them back very speedily. To my children, who were such a delight to spend time with in their growing years and have given us the joy of themselves plus seven grandchildren. Special thanks to my husband, who has given me unrestricted time to work on the book, with endless encouragement throughout.

1

AN INTRODUCTION TO COUNSELLING CHILDREN

Overview

Counselling children and adolescents can be the most difficult and the most rewarding work. Anyone who comes alongside a child who has experienced a traumatic event in life is affected by the encounter. However, most children grow and mature in a healthy enough way to withstand the difficulties that confront them, so it is good for therapists to remember the healthy majority, as it is all too easy to think that the children who need specialist help are the norm. Working with those who suffer most must not blind us to the fact that children can be resilient and survive many traumas without our interventions. We look first of all at the general world of counselling and the place of child therapy.

The importance of counselling

Counselling children and adolescents is of vital importance in today's world. Children and young people face challenges in many areas of their lives – at home, at school, and in wider society. Each child has a unique story and unless the child can gain meaning from that story, the world can be a frightening place in which to live.

Fortunately there are many children and young people who are able to grow and develop healthy emotional personalities. Growing up is never a smooth ride, but the majority of our children are able to emerge with resolve and purpose to take their place in society.

This book addresses the problems of the minority of children and young people for whom the struggle is too great and who need help to overcome the distress and pain that have impeded their emotional growth. They do not see their problems as something alien, as this is their experience; it is just how life is. To the adult generation, there are past experiences with which to compare the present, and decisions can be made on the evidence. For the child, the reservoir of experience is so much smaller, and new events need interpreting. The child may find no relief for all the feelings that are stirred up and unless help is available promptly, the child can act out his feelings or withdraw, which can hamper his life for many years.

It is a fact that children need help for many different problems in their lives.

In 1999, the UK Office for National Statistics stated the following facts:

- 10 per cent of all children will need some kind of mental health intervention during their school lives. Among children aged 5–15, 5 per cent had clinically significant conduct disorders, 4 per cent had emotional disorders (anxiety and depression) and 1 per cent were hyperactive; 0.5 per cent of the sample suffered from less common disorders such as autistic spectrum disorders and eating disorders. The overall rate of mental disorders among the sample was 10 per cent, but this included some children who had more than one disorder.
- More boys than girls had mental disorders (11 per cent and 8 per cent, respectively); this difference holds even controlling for age. The gender difference was also apparent among those with conduct disorders and hyperkinetic disorders, but not among those with emotional disorders, where there was no gender difference.
- Black children were more likely to have a mental health problem (12 per cent) than white children (10 per cent), Pakistani and Bangladeshi children (8 per cent) and Indian children (4 per cent).[1]

The need for counselling children will increase; if children are not helped when they are young, their emotional health will be compromised and they will not have the opportunity to develop healthy relationships. Any child who has experienced a traumatic event in life needs help. If that help can be given in the home, by loving parents, supported by friends, or contained by a community that cares, then that is the best answer to his need. But when those resources are not available, then the child needs to have somebody who can listen, somebody who can contain the unspeakable pain, somebody who can sustain a relationship with the child, no matter how difficult. There will also be those children who have very loving parents who find that a child of theirs comes up against a problem that they cannot understand or contain, and they are only too ready to seek help for their children from a professional who can share the burden and use more than parenting skills to find the deeper significance of inexplicable behaviours.

If a child's needs for counselling can be met at the onset of any problems, there is much greater hope of resolution. Children learn how to defend themselves against unbearable pain. The more time there is for those defences to be consolidated, the longer it will take for the child to allow someone to get behind the defences and find the real person.

Relating is a human thing to do. When pictures were shown of Romanian orphans left in homes to be physically cared for, but receiving no interaction with other people, everyone could see that the children were not able to grow normally in any way. Communication with other humans is vital for the growth of the human child.

John Bowlby's attachment theory has been hugely influential; Bowlby disagreed with Freud's contention that a baby seeks its mother's company in the early days of life simply to receive instinctual gratification, including food, from her. Instead, Bowlby postulated that, in fact, the baby is seeking to attach itself in a relationship with a person to receive safety, comfort and communication. He felt that the quality of the relationship that developed between the child and its mother laid down the blueprint for all later relationships. If the child was securely attached to its mother, then the child would be capable of making other secure relationships at all stages of life. This meant he would manage school alliances and later be able to have an intimate relationship with another person, able to set up a new family group. This has its roots in early feelings. If love and hate are negotiated in the child's early life, then there will be no need for the child to become violent. If the child feels that he is acceptable as a person, he will treat others as also acceptable. Meaningfulness in relationship is an important part of this. Meaningfulness gives *raison d'être*. It is difficult to progress meaning unless there is a paradigm that gives some shape to making sense of the world and interacting with it. That requires consistency.

Child therapy

It is difficult to describe therapy for particular age ranges, as every child and adolescent is a unique person. There has been some innovative psychotherapy work suggested that enables a newborn baby to be represented by another therapist, while the mother is receiving her own therapy. Generally for the child to be seen as the client on his own, the child needs to be able to communicate in some way with another person. Children of three are often able to do this, but a child of lower age might be able to use counselling.

Play therapy is suitable for children aged 3 to around 11. Again, there will be some children who would rather talk than play before 11. There are also older children who have missed out on play in their younger years and therefore benefit from a playroom environment. It is a frequent occurrence, particularly for children in residential care, to benefit from play activities when they are 14 or 15. The whole of the child's development pattern needs to be taken into account and no rules developed for including or excluding children and young people from specified pursuits.

Young people mature at different times in their teenage years. The Royal College of Psychiatrists has defined adolescence in the UK as from around 11 years for girls and 13 for boys. The USA suggests figures lower than these. The majority of young people over the age of 16 would be more likely to want to talk rather than play; however, drawing, writing and doodling are often activities that are chosen ways of working for those in later adolescence and some adults.

There are many books written on counselling, and training manuals abound for students studying on proliferated courses. The vast majority of these are directed towards work with adults. There are many issues that encourage people to seek personal help and adult therapy interventions are now accepted, but there is more reluctance to accept that children suffer difficulties, which can be as serious and distressing as those of an adult. Children need counselling to enable them to overcome the experiences that have damaged them, so that they can grow into adulthood in a healthy way. Otherwise, the child has to find coping mechanisms that will deny him the opportunity to develop his real self.

Wherever possible help should be given in the child's family setting with people who are committed to the child's best interests. But there are times when the child's parents/carers are unable to cope with the distress the child experiences. This can occur when the other family members are also caught up in the suffering or where the resources are inadequate to deal with the situation. Too often, the pain that adults feel denies that children experience the same pain. Sometimes there is the casting aside of the child's needs as 'the child is too young to understand' or 'we will not talk about it in case the child gets upset'. Both of these ideas allow no place for the child to have his own feelings. In order to keep the adults' equanimity, they fail to permit the child to work through his hurt.

Generally, many clients attending counselling centres come from a 'family' background; counsellors working in schools and special provision establishments may deal with children from foster homes and other placement provision. Then there are those specialist counsellors who work in clinical settings where the children they see are in residential placements.

Society in general likes the idea that childhood is the happy time of candyfloss, ice-cream, laughter and innocence, but it is impossible to hold to this image if reflection is used at all. For a whole variety of reasons, children today have less stability in their lives than children of previous generations. Life has never been easy for children, as there are difficulties to be faced both within the immediate group in which they are raised and in the prevailing social, economic and political environment.

Early relationships

The quality of relationship between a child and its first carer has been documented widely (see Stern,[2] Winnicott,[3] Bowlby,[4] Brazelton & Cramer[5]). Because the child has had an experience *in utero* for nine months before birth, this has to be considered as the first relationship. Many children who have been given up at birth for adoption and have adequate care still have a feeling that somehow they were not good enough to be loved.

Children cannot invest in deep relationships unless the significant persons to whom they are relating give a consistent pattern of caring over time. A child who experiences rejection by a loved parent will not easily trust another adult. Rejection is not easily overcome; to be let down is to feel an unworthiness of being loved. It is not the truth of the situation, but the child feels that he is instrumental when close family ties loosen. Too often adults fail to appreciate that a child has only a limited experience of life and therefore any major changes in the family cause the child enormous insecurity. Adults can become impatient with children who cannot adjust to their choices, as though the child were deliberately trying to be awkward and disruptive. The fact is that the child has been disrupted and needs time and understanding to come to terms with new relationship situations.

The child cannot invest in a new relationship to the same degree as he did with the first relationship. After a point of relationship crisis, the child cannot go to a deeper level of trust until he has tried and tested a new experience. Where he goes through serial relationship crises, the potential depth of relationship is likely to diminish.

Counselling as reparation

Counselling children and young people seeks to give the individual a new experience – a new way of relating. Children who have missed out, for whatever reason, on having somebody to protect them from the mass of experience that has rained down on them, need a way of relating that trusts another adult to give to them a reliable interpretation of what is happening to them in their specific situation.

CASE EXAMPLE

Diana

Diana was 8 years old when her mother brought her for therapy. Mother's concern had been over a period of time, but the intensity of Diana's violent outbursts towards others had been escalating and recently the child had beaten up a smaller child for no apparent reason. Also, mother was of slight stature and Diana was becoming increasingly strong. In a play fight, Diana had pinned her mother to the floor and mother declared that she had been unable to get up. She had found a joking way out of the situation, but was now terrified that the child might soon be able to physically attack her. The head teacher at Diana's school had discussed with the parents suspending the child for her acts of aggression towards several children prior to this event. Diana was a very bright child and had no problems with her school work; she had not experienced bullying from other children, but was seen as the school's worst offender.

When the therapist began work with Diana, Diana was able to talk about all kinds of everyday things, but did not want to talk about the difficulties. She said she felt that everyone picked on her and she was made the scapegoat for everybody's nastiness. The therapist felt that she was making no headway with the child, but noticed that after each session, when Diana's mother collected her, Diana would go towards her mother with her head down and then charge at her mother's abdomen.

After many sessions, Diana curled up in a large, black leather chair. The therapist commented that the child looked very comfortable. Diana said 'I am safe in here.' The therapist suggested that perhaps outside the chair she might feel unsafe. Diana protested that she did not want to ever get out of the chair. She was in her Mummy's tummy and it was safe in there. She did not want to be born. The therapist suggested that it might be good for Diana to learn more about the time when she had been born. The therapist also wondered whether the charging at the mother was an attempt to portray that Diana would like to get back to being unborn. Diana agreed that she wanted to know about her birth and asked her mother to tell her. The therapist suggested that it could be done in a counselling session, so that she too might understand more of what went on.

At the next session, Diana's mother confirmed that she had never spoken to Diana about her birth. She admitted that she, herself, preferred not to think much about it, as it was a time of real difficulty. The therapist asked mother to go back to the time when she first knew that she was pregnant. Mrs T had been delighted; she had one son and was hoping that this baby would be a girl. She had been well during the pregnancy and all had gone according to plan. The day of delivery arrived. Mrs T went into hospital to have her baby and when it arrived, it was the girl she so wanted. She was delighted, but only for a few minutes. A doctor came to see mother and baby and was alarmed about the baby's health, so he took the baby away from her mother and disappeared. The baby Diana was then subjected to 12 injections within the next 24 hours and for two days was not seen or held by her mother. Diana sat thoughtfully throughout this description.

Mrs T expressed her sadness that her beautiful little girl had been taken away. The doctor came back and said that the baby was in intensive care, as he suspected the child had a severe heart complaint. Later, the diagnosis was found to be incorrect. Diana had a healthy heart. Mrs T. explained her grief and shed tears as she told Diana how distraught she was. Diana showed some concern for her mother.

When mother had left the session, the therapist asked Diana how she felt before she was born. Diana responded that she was safe and that being born had been very dangerous. She curled up again in the chair and the therapist suggested she might like to talk about being born, now she knew what had actually happened. Diana began with a repeat of the previous session, saying that she did not want to be born. When she had been born, her mother had let the doctors take her away and with all the injections those doctors had picked on her all the time. She had no Mummy to help her. Diana began to cry and to feel that the separation from her mother had been the unsafe part of being born. It was as though her mother had abandoned her to people who 'picked on her'.

After many weeks of working with this material, Diana began to appreciate something of her mother's feelings when she was born. She made the connection that her sadness and isolation were also experienced by her mother – that they were both sad at the same time and they both shared similar feelings.

When the work had been going on for more than a year, Diana stopped charging at her mother when she left the counselling room. Mother reported that Diana would now talk to her rather than ignoring everything she said. The head teacher had reported to the parents that Diana was now tolerating much more from her school peers and not retaliating, even in provocative situations.

Towards the end of the work with the therapist, Diana one day came out of her session and found her mother's hand and held it. There was a level of trust built between child and mother through a shared experience.

For many weeks of this work, the therapist had little understanding of what was causing the overwhelming feelings of Diana needing to attack people. When she curled up in the foetal position in the chair and spoke of being in her mother's tummy, Diana gave a clue as to when the trauma might have taken place. The child had never heard the story of her birth, but when she did, she was able to make sense of some of her feelings of attack towards her mother and towards other people. She had primitive feelings of her mother abandoning her; for the child it was her reality and any threat of being abandoned again by mother or of being 'picked on' by anyone else reactivated those feelings. She had no way of thinking through what was happening, as she did not have the story. But her feelings leaked out and she had to defend herself against the intolerable pain she had felt at birth. The feelings her mother experienced had never been part of the picture, as they were totally hidden. Mother found it difficult to communicate well with her daughter, as Diana had the threat of abandonment within her. She needed a third adult to intervene, with whom she could build up the trust that had fractured between herself and her mother at her birth. Once this trust was built with the therapist, Diana could transfer to a relationship with her mother, whom she then saw as suffering in the same way as she herself had suffered. Her mother had not wilfully given her to other people who would hurt her. One can imagine that going to school aged 5 would have been another indication to Diana's schema that mother was abandoning her to another group of people; especially as at that time another baby was born into the family.

The new counselling relationship enabled Diana to work out in a new dynamic the interplay between herself and a caring adult. The therapist was always mindful that the resolution needed to be in the child being able to transfer the trusting relationship back to her mother.

Some children have not had the environmental factors that have nurtured emotional growth. Where this has been lacking, counselling offers the opportunity of a new way of working with a trained professional, who sees the child's need as paramount, and as soon as trust has been established will be working towards the resolution of the areas of conflict in the child's life, by linking back to the person originally involved. Sometimes the other person is not able or not willing to rebuild. Sadly, the child's reparative approaches may be spurned. Where it is attainable, this will free the child to develop in other relationships without the encumbrance of past events still pulling back the child's emotional reactions to a previous time.

Counselling as self-development

Every child needs to develop his own individuality. Counselling enables emotionally vulnerable children to come to know themselves as they really are and to enable those selves to grow and develop to the maximum potential possible within the constraints placed upon them. It helps them to accept their strengths and their weaknesses and to work towards fulfilment, building on their strengths and accommodating their weaknesses. It is the ability to hold the ambivalences of life that enables children to become rounded individuals. Counselling cannot necessarily take away the things that stand in the path of some children, but it can empower children to do the best within the set of life circumstances in which they find themselves.

Donald Winnicott wrote a great deal about 'the facilitating environment', by which meant that the child, who grew in an environment in which he was appreciated and his emerging ideas valued, would develop a healthy sense of self. Counselling can provide a setting in which a child, who has been deprived of a nurturing setting, can discover his competencies and try them out in a conducive atmosphere of acceptance.

There are a number of children whose behaviour does not permit them to function well in society. We shall look at behaviours from a psychodynamic perspective, which views behaviours as having their origin in earlier emotional experiences, which have been unprocessed and are locked into the unconscious. When triggered, the feelings associated with the past events erupt in actions that would have been appropriate in the previous situation, but do not fit the current circumstances. This book will give examples of how therapists have enabled children to make links with past events in their lives and have then been able to change their reactions from within.

The therapeutic alliance

How the therapist makes a link with the child client is extremely important. The child must feel contained for any work to be done. But containment is more than being able to cope with the child. It is a two-way process; the child has to be able to trust enough to use the containing person. There are two ways of responding to a child; the 'oppositional' position and the 'alongside' position. In the 'oppositional' position, the therapist believes that there are difficulties which prevent the child from growth; these difficulties arise from the child's inner experience. In the 'alongside' position, the therapist believes that the child is capable of emotional growth and that within the therapy there will be a natural forward movement. The difficulties lie in external disturbances which have hindered the child. The task then is to clear the obstacles so that the child can make progress. Lavinia Gomez has written a fascinating article on this, describing both approaches and their pitfalls.[6] These two positions need not be mutually exclusive; the difficulty is in trying to use both positions when necessary without confusing the two. They need to be held in tension, but not muddled. Working with children means that some of the time the counsellor will be the adult who needs to challenge, 'opposite' the child; at other times the child's adult playmate, 'alongside' the child. The distance between client and therapist has to be not too far away as to have no connectedness, but not so close that the child sees the therapist as a parent substitute or an extension of himself that he can subsume into himself. Each child will need to do all he can to find the person of the therapist. The therapist does not reveal personal material, but has to be real with the child. This is to be a new relating experience.

There has to be playfulness; therapy takes place in the space which connects the child and the therapist. In play therapy, the objects the child uses become the medium through which communication takes place. Unless the therapist can respond in a like manner to the child's contribution, the child will feel that the connection has not been made.

Playfulness is an antidote to the therapist defending herself against pain. If the pain is present in the room, it can be faced; if it is excluded, there is no way of dealing with it. To stay with a child's pain is not easy; it causes distress in both parties. It is in the sharing of it that new feelings of being held can emerge. The therapist holds the child's pain and gradually feeds it back in small quantities. The therapist needs to deal with her own pain by sharing it in supervision.

The playing and the sharing are an important part of the alliance. It is how the therapist is with the child and who the child perceives her to be. There needs to be ingenuous receptivity at the level of the child's play that accepts everything that the child shares; it is held to be important and a special treasure to retain until the next meeting.

Much reflective scrutiny needs to follow the play session. In thinking about the spoken and unspoken messages that came from the child; in pondering the feelings that were present in the room; in wondering what main themes were expressed; all these deliberations will help to formulate hypotheses that may help in future work. There is a great deal that needs to be stored in the therapist's absorbed way of thinking.

Summary

1. We looked at the importance of counselling for children.
2. Early relationships are vital, as they set the pattern for future social interaction.
3. Counselling can help children in a compensatory way, when they have missed out on dependable care.
4. Counselling can also assist children's self-development.

2
EMOTIONAL DEVELOPMENT

Overview

Having looked at the wider world of counselling, we now look particularly at the emotional development in the young and maturing child. We look at some of the theories about the maturation of children, noting the contributions of Donald Winnicott, Erik Erikson and John Bowlby. Theories are useful as long as we do not try to fit children into the theories, but work with the child as he presents and use theory as a tool for understanding the presentation.

Human patterning

The child therapist needs to be aware of the healthy emotional development of children. The emotional life of the child is above all relational: a child cannot grow in the affective domain unless there is interaction with other human beings. Every child needs models from which to form an idea of how to experience life – the human child needs to copy human behaviour from human models. The child tries to do what he *sees* others doing; tries to make the sounds he *hears* others making; tries to *smell* things that he sees others smelling; tries to put anything in his mouth to *taste;* and wants to touch and be touched. He experiments with all these senses, learning that they can give pleasure or disgust. He creates patterns of like or dislike, so that after repeated experiences of the feeling towards particular things, the child learns to reach out to pleasurable things and to withdraw rather than to interact with things that disgust. These movements are based on the child's own set of sensory feelings. For example, one child may love the feel of velvet, whereas another may cringe and refuse to touch it.

The human child needs to recognize what other human beings do and how they behave, in order to have examples of how things might be in the future as they become more competent.

It is true that competencies can be taught to a child and the education system is often seen as the imparting of knowledge, commonly known as 'the jug and mug' method. The teacher is the possessor of knowledge, which she then seeks to deposit in the child. To meet the current demands of the curriculum, teachers have little space for creating a learning environment in which the child's natural curiosity leads him to explore and seek out his own answers to his inquisitiveness.

CASE EXAMPLE

Amanda

Amanda was the 7-year-old daughter of a sculptor; she attended a school which catered for children whose parents were professionals of some standing. The curriculum was geared to getting as many children as possible to junior public schools when they were 9.

Towards Easter, the teacher of Amanda's class gave each child a cardboard egg holder, some yellow and green gummed paper and a white card. The children were to create a spring card. The teacher drew a daffodil on the blackboard and explained that the egg carton was to be used as the flower's trumpet. Amanda produced her flower and then made very decorative leaves that curled around her flower. When the teacher saw this, she scolded Amanda, saying that the curled leaves 'were not daffodil leaves' and therefore unacceptable.

It is questionable as to what the teacher was trying to achieve. Probably she wanted 25 cards, all very similar, that portrayed as accurately as possible a real daffodil. However, if she wanted a child's work of art, the one who achieved the most artistic effect was Amanda. But rather than encouraging the child's creativity, the teacher stifled it. There was imposition rather than expression. Conformity was valued above originality.

Conformity

Conformity is seen as success. When children conform, they are thought of as 'normal'; the difficulty with this is that conformity is the outward manifestation of accepting principles laid down by others. Without some rules, there would be anarchy; however, the greatest reforms have come about because there were those who resisted being poured into the mould of those around them. At a political level, it is the question of freedom fighter or guerrilla – apartheid in South Africa would not have ended without the strength of those who held to their beliefs in spite of the prevailing harshness of the regime that tried to suppress their values. For the child, it is whether to comply against his inner passion or to resist the authority and carry out his own desire. The child first meets this conflict of interests in the toddler stage, as will be discussed later.

It is possible to change behaviours in certain ways. A behaviourist view would assert that the best way of dealing with unwanted behaviours is to eliminate them by a programme of retraining. Children can be threatened or bribed. In modelling conduct, behaviour therapy seeks to reinforce good behaviours by rewarding them and to eliminate bad behaviours by punishing them. These are known as positive and negative reinforcers. These come from an external locus and the internal events of emotion, beliefs, previous experience and instincts are not taken into account.

When the child is learning from his own experience, he is able to make choices. Each child can make up his own mind as to whether a thing is good or bad for him. The selection is made internally; thus the locus of control is within the child, but then needs to be communicated and expressed externally to others.

A key issue is that of respect. If an adult respects the child, the child is likely to respect the adult and a relationship is forged. If the adult assumes a right to respect in excess of that which is willingly offered to the child, there is more likely to be conflict. The value of each child is in who he is rather than in what he can achieve.

Pre-birth experience

In fact, a baby is born with several experiences already in place. It is known that babies in the womb can suck their thumbs; certainly they know how to suck to remove their hunger when they are newborn. They can hear from around 22 to 24 weeks;[7] they experience the difference between light and darkness at 6 months. Foetal experience is every bit as important as the early months of life. Already the child is picking up information from the mother. The relationship that is made with the mother seems to be from an early stage of pregnancy.[8] A child has feeling capacity long before it can express the feelings in words or actions.

There is a great deal of anxiety over what pregnant women should eat and how they should prepare for the birth and a plethora of information about all the physical details. But there is little concern given to help mothers understand that their attitude towards the unborn child can have a huge effect on the baby's developing emotions. Many a child who was not wanted goes through life aware of the fact and may display in later years a need to castigate himself. There are various difficulties that arise during a pregnancy and a pregnant mother cannot be glowing all the time. No harm comes to foetuses when there are occasional incidents of exasperation, tiredness and anger. It is the overarching experience that gives the child the sense of well-being or of disappointment. The child who is longed for and waited for with great anticipation is the child who will thrive and feel that being born is to be welcomed by close kindred. Where this does not occur, the child can feel that being born is to face hostility and that sense can be hard to modify.

CASE EXAMPLE

Billy

Mr and Mrs A. had decided that their lifestyle was to be on their own; they would not have children. They were both in professional work and had made many plans of all that they could achieve. They would have a high-profile social life; the husband wanted to extend his hobby of scuba-diving by diving in exotic places. His wife wanted to further her career and to make a better home in the country, giving full rein to all her ideas for the interior decoration of the house. She then became pregnant; this was a dilemma; she did not believe that abortion was right for her, but neither did she want to give up her dreams. Her husband was annoyed about the pregnancy and would have agreed to a termination if his wife was willing. Early on he began to shout at the child, telling it that it had messed up all his plans. When Billy was born, the parents took good care of the baby physically, but there was resentment about having to curtail their own way of living and having to put the baby's needs before their own. Later the child was referred to a child psychotherapist, because the child was not confident and tried to hide away from people. At playgroup, he would not play with other children, but wandered off to a secluded area and sat listlessly in the corner. Billy seemed to be trying to stay out of the way, afraid of intruding into anybody else's space. As he grew up he could never believe that other children wanted him to play with them. If an adult spoke crossly to him or there was any shouting, he shut his eyes tightly and cowered.

This little boy seemed to understand that he had intruded into an environment where he was not really welcome. Billy attributed to others the lack of welcome he had experienced before his birth. Although his parents amply provided for his physical needs, emotionally they were distanced from him. As he became more competent, the parents began to enjoy him more, as he required less of their time, but the child remained isolated among his peers. Events from before birth can have an impact on the emotional development of children.

Some pregnant mothers spend hours thinking about what their baby will be like. In a survey,[9] mothers spoke of the physical features they imagined their children would have at birth, about the likes and dislikes they had interpreted from their babies' reactions when they ate certain foods, and one mother swam every day to be like her baby who was 'swimming' in the amniotic fluid. Another mother spoke of how she felt that her baby could know about the things she herself was experiencing, so when she was looking at a horse, she believed that the image of the horse would travel along the neurons and would reach the foetus's central nervous system and so convey that image to her baby. This is what Winnicott called the mother's 'reverie'[10] and created the relationship between mother and foetus. The child is in the mother's mind and treated as though it were already a person. There is much debate about when a foetus becomes a baby and whether at conception it is a lump of tissue or a human being, but once the child is recognized as having an existence, it is endowed with personhood.

Alessandra Piontelli[11] used ultrasound scans to monitor the activities of babies before they were born. She then visited the children over a period of time until they were 4 years old. She was amazed by the behaviours that she witnessed before birth and the subsequent continuation of those behaviours.

Thomas Verny and John Kelly[12] have written a great deal about the traumas unborn children suffer and how those traumas can be relived in a child's feelings. They cite instances of adults who have experienced knowing facts that parents had not disclosed to them. In one case, a musician was intrigued by his ability to know the score for the cello in the music he was conducting before he turned the page. The mystery was solved when his mother told him that the pieces he knew were the ones she herself had been rehearsing on the cello when she had been pregnant.

The first carer

When a baby is born, it is still in some senses merged with its mother. Winnicott said: 'There is no such thing as a baby.'[13] We know that is not strictly true, but the point that Winnicott was making was that a child cannot survive without a carer. The baby is helpless to meet any of its own needs. It has to be fed, to be kept safe and comfortable; but that is not all. A baby needs emotional nurture as much as physical nurture. Just as a child will die if it does not have the basic physical environment, so a baby dies emotionally unless there is a 'good-enough'[14] emotional facility.

Physical growth is easily seen and concerns are quickly raised if a child does not reach the normal milestones of physical development. Emotional stunting is far less apparent, but just as serious in the young child. Healthy emotional growth will enable a child to learn, to make relationships, to find his place in the world, to understand commitment to work and to play, in fact to balance all the facets of his life, so that life can be well spent.

The first person who gives the child any sense of self is the main carer. As the infant gazes into the face of the one who nurses him, he looks for a response. If the response is positive, the child engages more and more in interaction, gaining esteem from the feedback. If the response is negative, the child will either seek for more attention to try to get some interaction acknowledged, or will give up on the carer and distance himself from her. Where communication is established, the child has a frame of reference in which he plays a part. The games that mothers and babies develop have been well documented by various writers.[15]

The newborn child needs love and the only way that a baby can experience love is in being held close to somebody, in being nurtured by being in contact and communication; the child may not understand the language but he experiences the warmth. The caring adult speaks to the child as if the child could understand. The child will respond to those who nurse it and most parents eagerly await the day when their baby will return a recognisable smile. How does a baby learn to smile? It is a mutual admiration. The baby sees pleasure in the mother's face and the baby feels good. He responds with a smile, which gives the mother more pleasure. She reveals to the child that she is pleased with him and this reinforces the baby's pleasure, and so the game goes on. The little child soon realizes that when he smiles, the mother will gain pleasure from his initiation of the game.

In a similar way, the child begins to give signals when things feel bad. When the baby is hungry he yells. The 'good-enough mother' (a term used by Winnicott) comes to the small baby quickly, so that she can relieve the distress that the baby has signalled. She will soothe him and feed him, if that is the problem. Or it may be that the child's nappy needs to be changed. The baby soon learns that to cry is to bring the caring mother to his aid and to make it better. Emotionally, the baby is learning the pattern that pleasure can be a shared social experience and that mother is willing to help when he has a problem. The child has only to put out the signal and it is heeded. In the early days of life, the child needs an adult to be thinking about his needs and making sure they are met. It is in this very early stage that trust develops. The caring parent cannot be available for the child at all times in all circumstances, but the child needs a general experience of having his needs met, to sense that there is reliability in this new world and that generally other human beings care for each other. This first experience of trust enables the child to develop his own ability to have confidence in others.

One of the tasks of the first carer is to give the child experiences that are consistent enough to allow him to build up a pattern of how the world is and to contain anything that would disrupt the child's forming ideas. It is through memory that a child learns to anticipate, and anticipation is essential in keeping unmanageable anxiety at bay. For the child who has no sense at all of predictability, the world and everyone in it is exceedingly frightening. Anything could happen at any time and there is nobody to whom to turn who will calm any fears. In its extreme form, a child has no sense of integration; there is no shape to memory and life is a nightmare. The only defence is to fight it and to attack everyone and everything before people and/or things attack the individual. The high state of anxiety and the desperation felt give the child no option but to abreact. An experience of predictability is the only way in which a child learns to understand and interpret the environment for himself. Otherwise the child learns that life is chaotic.

It is as if the caring adult holds an umbrella over the child, to protect the child from the raining down of new experience, until such time as the child is able to hold his own umbrella. Even then, there may be new showers of experience that threaten to turn the child's umbrella inside out and then the child knows that the adult can be trusted to hold a mitigating protection until he is able again to weather the new happening. Time after time this happens and the child learns to integrate all the experiences into one whole pattern of life. It is not that everything is repeated, but there is enough familiar patterning for the child not to feel frightened. The child will then go out to explore other things, being assured that there will always be a place of safety to which to return, when things seem to overwhelm. If the protection is not there and the child is left to be the recipient of the deluge of experience without a mediator to interpret, the good experiences can be collected in the memory, but the unacceptable things cannot be held at all and so are banished from the conscious mind. This is like a pool of unintegrated events, which are too scary for the child even to contemplate. It would be good to think that these things could be banished, but they cannot be evacuated from the child's psyche. Instead they reside as unconscious fears and threats, a pool of unexpressed emotion. The ego may form an adapted presentation to the world, with no acknowledgement of the inner pain and terror that is unintegrated. But from time to time, the waters of the pool are disturbed by a trigger that resembles something that was a past uninterpreted event. Then the waters erupt and the ego cannot keep the flood under control.

Children are often seen as unable to control themselves and often labelled as 'out of control'. But they have no hope of controlling something that has made them feel in fear of annihilation. Behaviour always has an origin, but because children are unable to give words to the threats that overwhelm, they can only act out the way that they feel. Freud talked about repression, those feelings that need to be put into a place that does not threaten existence. Repressed feelings do surface. Often the traumas children faced were before they had the vocabulary to put their feelings into words, but the feelings remain active. This activity shows in an eruption of feeling that gives relief to the anxiety built up within the child.

When the baby is born, he becomes totally dependent on another person taking care of him. Just as he has been carried and fed before birth, so he now has to be in the mind of a caring adult for his needs to be met. Where the primary needs of the child are generally not met, or where there is no consistency in the way the baby is handled, then the baby cannot develop the pattern of trust. Anxiety sets in and each event is a new experience and yet another confusion.

As the infant and mother adjust to each other, there comes a time when the 'good-enough mother' knows that she does not have to respond immediately to her child. She knows that the child will trust her enough to come to his help before desperation sets in. So she lets the child cry for a couple of minutes, often calling out that she will come soon. The child is reassured and mother comes. Gradually the child knows that delay in the mother's coming does not mean anything dreadful. She will come to him. She comes and all is well. He is learning to tolerate frustration. The child is going to meet frustration in many different guises; he is learning that mother does not have to be in sight all the time, but she can be relied upon to turn up.

The therapist as carer

The therapist always cares about the child, but where there has been difficulty in the relationship between the child and his primary carer, the therapist will need to become a substitute significant person in rela-tionship, without usurping the primary carer's place in the child's life.

When the child therapist meets a child, there is likely to be a period of mistrust, while the child tests out whether or not the therapist is reliable. Trust is the first thing that has to be established. Caring for the child is not in the same role as the parent, but where there has been disappointment, the new relationship with the therapist is an attempt to build a different way of relating. Many counsellors, especially in the early stages of counselling a child, are too eager 'to do something' or to get the child to achieve something. This pressure is felt by the child, who may become anxious to please, but the anxiety hinders any real work being done. Trust is fragile and needs plenty of time to develop. Being present with the child, giving him full attention, without any pressure, is the way to allow the child to find his own way to trusting the adult.

Occasionally a child will create a relationship with the therapist with an uncanny immediacy. There are children who are so desperate to trust someone, because their previous experience has been that trust has been betrayed. But they do not enter into a real relationship. As a defence, they build up a strategy of meeting every new person with the false hope that this person will be the one who will provide the real caring, but underlying this profuse introduction lies fear. The child is looking for a carer who can be like a mother at birth, who will answer every need. This is not possible for any adult. The therapist needs to work with the child through times of disappointment on both sides. The therapist cannot work as though the child has established true trust, ignoring the underlying fearful aspects of the child. The trust that is built has to be real, which means the fear has to be recognized and the child helped to see that relationship is only possible on honest terms. The fear can be acknowledged.

As the child develops trust, that is the springboard for the relationship to progress. There are times when the therapist allows the child some disappointments and does not accept all his demands. She allows some frustrations to occur and helps the child to weather them. The child needs to experience that relationship can endure when things are not entirely satisfactory.

CASE EXAMPLE

Emma

When Emma was born, her mother was unable to look after her. There had been no prior plan for adoption, though Emma's mother felt that adoption would be the best for her baby. Emma was taken from her mother on her first day of life and later described herself as lying in a cot in a row of 12 babies.

She had been adopted by a couple when she was 6 months old and stayed with the family until she was 18.

Emma lived in constant fear of being rejected by any person in whom she put her trust.

At 15, Emma built up a relationship with a therapist. She hated the times when the therapist had to miss a week because of holidays. On one occasion, after having missed a session, Emma refused to leave the counselling room. The therapist told Emma that the session must end, but Emma persisted. The therapist left the room, reminding Emma that the session was at an end and that she should leave when she felt able to do so.

Emma sat in the counselling room by herself for 10 minutes and then left quietly. The therapist took this up in the following session, when Emma described how she had felt, for the first time in her life, that she had been able to avoid being pushed out from a safe place. She had only needed permission to stay and within 10 minutes she had been able to savour a new feeling of not being rejected.

This episode opened the way for Emma to talk about how she had felt pushed out and rejected by her mother. She knew little of her birth story, but she was well aware of her feelings. The feelings had been with her throughout her life and she trusted nobody until that deep hurt had been addressed. Once trust had been established, Emma was encouraged to hold herself during the times, such as holiday breaks, when she felt that she would lose the relationship. After such a break, Emma wrote these words which she handed to her therapist at her final session about a year later.

> Where are you now?
> What are you doing?
> Why does time exist?
> To separate
> So that I miss you and want to be with you.
> To be with you in the comfort and
> Refuge of your room.
> To hear your voice gently telling me
> It will be alright
> That you will give me all the time I need.
> You will not force me out and away from you
> Before I am ready.
> So that now, for once,
> My life will not be a case of survival,
> But will begin to be a pleasure.
> It will be like a sapling

Rooted deep
In reassurance
Confidence
And support.
With the gentle rain
Of care
Tenderness
And love
At long last washing over my upturned face.

You have helped me dare to believe
That something beautiful
Could finally grow and break free
From the tangle of thorns that held me captive
And that were my inheritance.
If you believe in me,
I can believe in myself.
If you have hope in me
I too, have hope for the future,
For new beginnings,
New life,
New joy.
I am no longer stumbling alone
Much afraid in the dark engulfing tunnel
That was my life –
You have taken my hand
And I have trusted you.
Together we are walking through
The painful shadows of my past.
You do not push me along in haste
But allow me to pick my way through
The boulders
Where fearful spectres hide.
You wait patiently
As I clamber the steep slopes of
Uncertainty –
Sometimes I stumble and fall back,
But you help me
To go ever onward and forward at my
Own pace.
And, with time, we will emerge from the dark tunnel
Into a bright meadow

Full of light and promise.
You will say to me 'Goodbye'
And I will be sad to lose you
But I will be richer for having known you
And for having allowed myself to
Trust you.

This shows how Emma used her thoughts to write down what was happening at the time of the break in counselling; she showed that she was able to hold herself and, for the first time, she was daring to look to a future when she would be able to manage without her therapist. Had there been no break and its disappointment for Emma, she would not have had the opportunity of working on her own and this gem of poetry might never have been written.

Erikson's epigenetic stages

Epigenetic refers to the idea that there is gradual development and organization as a child matures. Neural pathways expand to allow the steady increase in skills. Erik Erikson employed a psychosocial developmental list of eight stages covering the lifelong maturing of the person.[16] At each stage, Erikson believed there was a task that needed to be encountered – depending on the outcomes of the various stages, the child would have a good or bad idea of life. Of course, the two ends of the spectrum which he postulated are unlikely to be seen, and each child will be somewhere along the line. The opposing attributes must be seen as progression, rather than achieving one or the other extreme. The other difficulty with the model is that it suggests a step progression, as though the child was building a tower of bricks, putting one stage upon another. In reality, the steps overlap and each child's progress will be different. Because one stage is incomplete or negative does not mean that other stages have to wait or also have to be negative.

Erikson began thinking about life stages from the time of a baby's birth. Perhaps there should be inserted a stage prior to that, when the child is in the womb. The interaction between mother and foetus may be the starting point for the first stirrings of emotion in the child. Maybe the sense of belonging or rejection is acquired even this early.

Stage 1

The first task, for Erikson, in the infant stage, is described as the child developing trust. In the event that the child does not receive the care needed, he will grow with a mistrust of those with whom he has contact.

Normally, a child gradually builds up a sense of self from his own internalisation of the effects he has upon other people. If affirmation of the self is not given, then the child seeks it elsewhere. In many cases, other family members help to establish the self and later on peers and more external contacts encourage or discourage the formation of the child's personhood.

Stage 2

This stage Erikson described as accomplishing autonomy or engendering shame and doubt about the self. Once the child is sure of the attention that is given, he will want to explore new things. John Bowlby wrote about the secure base the child needs in order to move out into experience of his own.[17] A child who has had reliable parenting will happily play with a toy in a room by himself, as long as the adult is available. He can then go back to base for comfort or can cry out for help and the adult will appear. This requires the adult to be within earshot, giving enough attention to respond to the child. The child wants to try out his own thoughts and wants to do things in his own way. Temper tantrums ensue when he is not allowed to go ahead with his own plans. There is a battle of wills between parent and child. If the child is too much frustrated at this stage, he will have to make a choice. Either he will have to accept the parental interference and comply with the adult's wishes, or the child will have to follow his own desires and come into conflict with the parent. This is no easy matter for the child and this experience needs mitigation. If the child is true to himself, then the parent is going to be disappointed and maybe angry. The child feels that anger and disappointment can destroy the parent. But if the child chooses to please the parent, then he has to come to terms with the fact that his own thoughts are wrong and/or bad. To comply with the parent is to give up one's extended character in the shape of one's desire. Negotiation can be the best way forward. Where there is danger, the parent can give explanation as to why the child is prevented from carrying out his desires. Diversions to other things can make the child less threatened by adult intervention. Where a child is told 'No' at every attempt to fulfil his own ideas, he will often give up, and then creative and original thinking can be dulled or thwarted.

Given encouragement, the child will have enough sense of self to allow the space between himself and his mother to develop; no longer will the child see the mother as an extension of himself, but as a person in her own right. Where the separation does not take place, for whatever reason, the child develops a sense of shame. He remains in a contained relationship rather than holding himself.

The therapist will find that children vary in their presentation when this stage of development has not been negotiated well. Some children will present as looking to the therapist for permission to play, permission to move about the space, permission to speak. These are children who have capitulated to the carer's regime and decided not to challenge the set parameters. Other children will try to take charge of the counselling session. They will be so afraid that their ideas might be quashed at any moment, that they will not permit the space for the counsellor to comment or to be part of the play. There is an 'all-or-nothing' quality about these children. The therapist is aiming to get a therapeutic alliance with the child, so that in the earlier scenario the child is helped to take his own part in the session and in the latter case, the child is helped to be able to negotiate a role for the therapist. This needs to be done in a gentle, reassuring way, so that the child does not feel threatened. Such work may take a number of sessions.

Stage 3

Erikson suggested that at this stage the child would develop either initiative or guilt. This stage leads on from the new-found autonomy and has much in common with the previous one. The child who has developed ideas of his own will be seeking new ways to use those ideas. He will want to create imaginative environments and play out pictures of his mind's eye. Children who have established autonomy will have no problem enlisting other children to play *their* game. They are likely to be confident in carrying out tasks requested by others and will generally display a sense of self. Those who struggle with rigid rules from parents may need to be encouraged in new environments, as they may expect to be told what to do; whereas those who have not experienced boundaries at all will be at a loss when any suggestion is made to them. They will not be forthcoming with ideas of their own and may be fearful of making mistakes if others suggest activities to them, and so may be reluctant to start any endeavour.

In the counselling room, the child who has not successfully negotiated this stage may find it difficult to know how to proceed. He may look longingly at the materials provided, but be very reluctant to do anything. If the therapist suggests any activity, this may make him feel that the therapist has some expectation of him, which may make him fearful of failing to meet her hopes for him. He may fear punishment or ridicule if that has been his past experience. Therapists might be tempted to give lots of encouragement for the child to choose materials and to play, but even this might put more pressure on the child. Anxiety would then rise and the therapeutic value of the contact would diminish. Sometimes children need fewer choices, so that the materials on offer do not overwhelm. At the outset, it can be more productive to let the child explore the properties of the materials rather than use them. Commenting on colour, shape, sounds and texture can be less intimidating for the child who is nervous of his new surroundings. It is important that the therapist uses the vocabulary that can be shared with the client; a child with special needs calls for particular attention in this respect.

Stage 4

During the latency period, which covers generally the primary-school age, children create their attitudes towards work. Erikson put this in terms of developing industry or inferiority. School has a vital impact on their learning and the attitudes of parents towards their children's education are very influential. Parents who support their children's learning and help by interacting with the things that are happening at school are giving their children a head start, not only with what is learnt, but also with the inherent value of work.

Children who become intellectually curious enjoy discovering for themselves and become increasingly motivated to find out more. This affects how they get on at school. Children who find school work hard need encouragement, and those who can easily cope need to be given extra tasks to keep their minds hungry for new knowledge. As each child learns differently, there need to be plenty of resources. Firing children's imaginations is one of the greatest gifts that can be given for life.

If they receive positive feedback for their efforts at school and elsewhere, children will keep trying and enjoy their successes; but if they find criticism and belittlement is the reward for their labours, they will become unhappy and often try to find other ways of being accepted in their peer group. Feeling that they are not valued, they try to make others feel the same. Children may then give up on education. They decide that they cannot reach required standards and decide to cover their embarrassment in different ways. In primary school, some children volunteer to help in the classroom and like to stay behind to help the teacher. They are trying, in another way, to gain acceptance.

This often does not go down well with their peers and so they can become the butt of bullies. Some children feel angry with the children who can achieve and so victimize them. This takes many forms; it can be physical aggression, showing the bright child that the struggler is more competent in physical prowess; it may be verbal abuse, to try to do damage to the brighter child; or it may be unmerciful teasing and taunting. Another group of children decide that they are unable to make their mark by achieving results in school work, but they have a great desire to be liked by their classmates and they may become the class jokers. They make everyone laugh and when questions are being asked, they give amusing answers to disguise their lack of knowledge. Classmates encourage them as they laugh at their jokes.

So there are numbers of children who defend their inferior feelings by becoming people-pleasers, bullies or entertainers.

CASE EXAMPLE

Nadia

Nadia was a child who loved learning, but her school life became more difficult as she grew older. By the middle of secondary education, she was showing great promise for high grades in her examinations. She found it a constant struggle to keep at her studies. She was called 'boff' by her friends and watched television programmes that she disliked intensely simply to provide her with conversation in the playground. She was subjected to verbal bullying and a sense of being made to feel a freak. She wanted to be a lawyer and was focused on that goal. When her parents discussed her progress with teachers, the teachers intimated that Nadia was in advance of her years and was working at a level that would not be required until she was sitting external examinations. Some of her teachers' concerns were that Nadia might get bored with marking time and lose interest in the subjects in which she was doing well. The head teacher of the school waved aside the parents' concern, stating that the system had to be worked and there was nothing he could do to help Nadia fulfil her potential.

Nadia fulfilled her life's ambition and became a lawyer, but looked back on her schooldays as miserable. In her profession, Nadia felt that she had had to learn a whole new way of being that was foreign to her. Her social skills were underdeveloped by her schooling. Her own determination to succeed kept her going, but she felt her schooling had not given her encouragement and had let her down.

It is when children either cannot achieve or cannot be kept intellectually busy enough that they divert their interest. They may even be achieving very well, but if parents or teachers demand more than they can give, they have to find a defensive route for their energies.

Children who come for counselling during this stage often feel that they cannot compete with their peers. They become very unhappy at school and parents become aware of the distress of their child. A few children develop obsessional behaviours to keep everything under control. This may mask the feelings that they have of wanting to spoil things for others, so that those who are succeeding will understand how it feels to fail. They may become upset when asked to make decisions, for fear of making a wrong decision. Often they are afraid of making a mess and find that play is too fluid. They want to keep the room in order. At home they can find it all too difficult at times and then erupt into uncontrolled anger and distress.

In the counselling room, some of these children will want to defend themselves by pleasing the counsellor, being the bully, or come with a string of amusing stories or jokes. But underneath there may lie fears of being criticized by the therapist, or a relinquishing of all the authority to the therapist.

There may be times when management is appropriate, but showing stern authority is not helpful. The child needs to experience authority in a positive way. Children often play out school situations in which they take on teacher roles and show the punitive aspects of their authority. Discussion around such themes enables the child to work through some of his feelings about his successes and failings at school as well as at home.

There can be jealousy and rivalry between siblings over school work and sadly, teachers often make comparisons which can give a child feelings of inferiority.

Stage 5

As the child moves towards adolescence, there are all kinds of challenges to be faced. Erikson suggested that at this stage the young person would achieve an identity for himself or else be left with role confusion. The danger is that where a child has experienced unsatisfactory feedback, or not enough feedback, to feel any sense of the wholeness of his character, the adolescent will borrow from others and will take on an identity that is available. This may not be at all the desired personality, but needing some identity creates the desperation to hook into any identity that is available.

This identity is to be one's own, which means moving away from the identity that has been the accepted norm within the caring group, probably since the child was born. It depends how rigidly this family identity is held as to how difficult it will be to change. But the child has to emerge as a self that can stand by itself. Where this is not achieved, the child may want to merge with others in order to find some identity, but it will not be true to himself, but one borrowed from another person or a group of people. The child moves from the family identity to something else, but not a personal identity. The sad thing about this is that the adolescent is creating a false self.[18]

CASE EXAMPLE

Michael

Michael was 13 years old when his parents asked for him to be counselled. His father was quite non-communicative at the first interview and it was left to mother to explain the situation. Michael had allegedly been sexually abused by a teacher at his school, who had been suspended on account of this. Michael was not a child who often came to the notice of teachers, so this was taken very seriously. Mother wanted to make sure that her son now had the right help in order to overcome the terrible feelings which she thought would ensue.

The counsellor began to work with Michael. He had been brought up by fairly strict parents, but he had no real difficulty with that. He had recently joined a few friends from school who met together in the evenings and they smoked in secret. Michael knew that his parents would not welcome this behaviour, so he lied to them and would say he was going to a different friend's home to discuss homework. The sexual abuse did not seem to feature in Michael's mind at all and the counsellor, after a number of weeks, suggested that his mother had been mostly concerned with this incident that had not been discussed in their sessions. Michael became very reticent and said there was something that needed to be said, but for the next few sessions was unable to approach the issue. Then he declared that the sexual abuse never occurred; he was aware that a teacher had been suspended because of what he had said, there had been police involvement, social work reports and the family had been shattered. The counsellor spoke of Michael's need to have been part of the story and asked how he had become involved. Another boy at school had suggested that they did not particularly like one of the teachers. Michael had never experienced the teacher in any way that bred dislike from him personally, but he went along with the plan to concoct a story of abuse. Before he knew what would happen, he was embroiled in the story and felt he had to keep it up, as it felt to him that there was no way out. The momentum and attention he received from all the agencies kept him on a high. The other child involved had no qualms about the story and was pleased that he was able to influence the school enough to have the teacher suspended. The reaction of Michael was quite different. He realized that he was caught up in something that he wished he had avoided; now he wanted to put the record straight. He wanted the teacher to know he was sorry and that he knew he had acted in a wrong way.

Michael's need was born of a feeling that his parents could not give him any sense of his own identity and he borrowed an identity that did not fit him. Both his parents had their own problems of identity carried over from their own childhoods. Michael's mother acknowledged her own part in this and went through a course of therapy which benefited her greatly. Neither parent had a sense of his or her own individual worth and had been unable to emotionally respond to the needs of their child. So Michael, sensing that he had no identity that was recognisable, was looking for something that would give him a place in his society. He went along with a schoolmate, who had established himself with an identity. Michael did not want that identity, but in the absence of another, felt that anything that gave him a feeling of being somebody was better than nothing. There was a lot more work to be done with Michael. He had to face expulsion from the school and a new beginning in his school life. However, he was willing to rise to the challenges and to start to make his own choices. He had wanted attention from his father, but that was not available and so he had wanted to gain attention from a male authority figure. When drawn into the plan to hurt the teacher, there was something in Michael that wanted to say that he had a special relationship with a man. Sadly, his father was unable to face any of the issues of his own childhood, which might have helped him to understand more of Michael's feelings. Counselling enabled both son and mother to come to terms with who they were and their true identities.

The adolescent who cannot manage to work through to a point of finding an acceptable self will be confused as to how to present in the world. The young person may seek to opt out of the expected pattern of life and turn to alternative lifestyles in order to evade the responsibilities which confront the adolescent in passing from being a child to becoming an adult. Dependency on any substance can be used to avoid the pain of having to sort out values and belief systems. Personal relationships become difficult and there is the cycle of low self-esteem and lack of recognition that sets in. If the difficulties persist, the young person finds it difficult to break out of patterns that then label him.

Teenagers want to experience adults as having their own standards but not imposing these on them. They want to win the battles that ensue when there are differences of opinion. But they want to have the fight so that they can feel they gain the victory legitimately. If given free rein, they feel that they have not won their spurs.

Counsellors see quite a number of adolescents who are struggling with issues of finding identity. This may be expressed differently in many aspects of the teenager's life. There are sexual orientation issues, issues of school, examination choices, relationships with parents and peers, future career prospects, spirituality and values and a whole host of other thoughts and feelings which surge through the adolescent emotions. The therapist is there to help the young person steer his own course through a turbulent time, selecting the things from his background that he wishes to take with him into his adulthood and discarding those things that would hamper his maturity.

The growing-up process can give cause for the adolescent to feel that to engage with a therapist is to submit his hard-won individuality. Help with a specific aspect may be better tackled by short-term work, so that the young person does not feel too vulnerable. He can then get back on track with his peers without losing face.

CASE EXAMPLE

Dinah

Dinah was the daughter of a university professor and gained outstanding grades in her examinations. She was set to go to university, but decided not to continue studying hard for her entrance requirements. This was because the pressure put on her by her father meant that to go on succeeding academically was to submerge her own personhood in favour of her father's wishes. Dinah would have to renounce her own identity to conform, so she deliberately failed to do well enough at that stage to enter university. Dinah's father experienced frustration and expressed his anger to Dinah, as she was refusing to live out his image of her. She worked in a bookshop for a few years. Later on, in her own time, she went back to studying and gained university entrance. But this was not before she had cemented her own identity for herself.

Dinah wanted her father to acknowledge her growing independence and allow her to be responsible for her own learning. But he was unable to trust her to do this and made demands. The only way in which Dinah felt she could have any separate identity was to stop conforming to his rigid demands on her. Once her father had given up on her and expressed his disappointment, Dinah was able to reassess the situation in her own time and come back to do what she wanted to do, but without external pressure. She excelled at her course. No doubt her father was pleased too. But he had to recognise that it was her achievement and not his. Dinah created the space she needed to allow both father and daughter to recognise their separateness, which strengthened their relationship.

The further stages described by Erikson are briefly inserted to complete the picture.

Stage 6

Erikson has further stages – the young adult dealing with intimacy or isolation. Many teenagers try to deal with relationships by seeking an intimacy through sexual adventures. There are young people who dread isolation and therefore set up different alliances, some of which are healthy and some which lead them into trouble. For a young adult to achieve intimacy, he has to be able to share himself with another person at a deeper level of commitment. He will find difficulties if he has not found his own identity, as he will not know what he is wanting to share. For intimacy to occur, the young adult has to develop the capacity to be alone with himself, to be able to stand as a complete person who is not drawn to another by feelings of inadequacy.

The fear of isolation causes some young adults to foreclose ·on healthy group relations to set up with unsuited partners, only to discover that after a couple of years the commitment was premature. Some young people have been in such difficult circumstances that anything would feel as though it would be preferable. So they are unconsciously drawn to engage in relationships that meet an immediate need, but have no future.

Stages 7 and 8

Then comes middle age, when parents no longer have their children as dependents. Erikson suggests that at this point there needs to be new direction of interests to produce generativity or else the adult will fall into stagnation.

The last stage is old age, to be characterized by integrity. Integrity is described as having a satisfaction with the life one has lived. Erikson described the other end of the scale as despair – the regret over a wasted life with no time left to address any of the issues.

Winnicott

In a way similar to Erikson, Winnicott believed that there were tasks to be accomplished as a child grew towards maturity. He believed that it was in the nature of the child to mature, providing the environment and the mother figure allowed the potential to flourish.

Donald Woods Winnicott was a paediatrician who trained as a child psychotherapist. He was the first male child psychotherapist and was exceptional in many ways. He was greatly influenced by Darwin, Freud and Klein, but he preferred to examine and reflect on his practice before he thought about theories. He would often discover that the hypotheses which then came to him had already been formulated by others. However, there are many ideas that did come from his original thinking, which have been taken up by different professions. He did not put his ideas together as a theory, but from his writing and radio broadcasts, others have collected his work, which provides us with valuable insights. Michael Jacobs comments that Winnicott had various sequences of theory rather than a thread which linked them together. Winnicott often went much of the way with other theorists and then would give a distinctive twist in his explanations of phenomena. He spoke more about healthy development than about children's psychopathology.

His way of working was also influenced by Lord Horder, under whom Winnicott trained at St Bartholomew's Hospital. He always remembered the great surgeon telling his students to listen to their patients if they wanted to understand a situation. Winnicott made a lot of time to listen to children, but also to their parents in his trying to understand how he could best help a child. He geared all his attempts in practice to trying to understand and he used very ordinary language in his interactions, rather than using technical psychoanalytic terms. Some academics did not accept his views, but he was very popular with other groups. Probably, his radio broadcasts were successful because of his use of commonplace verbal skills.

Winnicott held that there was an ego from the beginning and that the child's existence was felt by being held by someone. The mother allows the baby to hold the illusion that he is at the centre of his world and that he has created what he needs; for example, he has created the breast that brings him food. The baby feels he is all one with the mother until such time as the mother allows the baby a tolerable space that is safe enough for him to allow her to be outside himself. This Winnicott referred to as the 'Me and Not-Me'. The ego then enables the internal self to relate to the external self. As the child adapts more to reality, he has to let go of the illusion of his merged self-and-mother.

The three stages of growth Winnicott identified as *absolute dependence, relative dependence* and *towards independence*. In the process of maturing, socialization would occur. In the first of these stages, the mother gives her undivided attention to the baby's needs; in the second stage, the mother purposefully allows her child to experience minor failures in her care for him. The child's anxieties are raised, but she is careful not to allow him too much frustration. Loss is a possibility when this stage is reached. Winnicott believed that absolute independence was not desirable, but as the child reaches towards independence, he is able to think about his mother and her return when she is absent, thus allaying fear. During this progression, Winnicott underlined the necessity for continuity of care, so that the child could experience reliable phenomena.

Winnicott believed that the child is born unintegrated; as he experiences a regularity of care, his ego-strength develops and he becomes integrated. This means he becomes a person in his own right and is able to relate to other objects. There are losses and gains throughout this process. The child returns to a state of unintegration when he rests or when there are no challenges to meet. But if the child is traumatized, then disintegration may take place. The child's integration can fragment. The earlier the impingement on the child, the more severe will be the disintegration.

Klein wrote about reparation, how the young child reaches a point of wanting to restore the relationship by making amends for what he feels he has destroyed, out of concern for the lost object. Winnicott maintained that the child could only develop guilt if there was the opportunity for reparation or constructive effort to rebuild. He preferred to attribute to the young child the 'capacity for concern' rather than call it guilt.

Winnicott argued that mental illness was a failure of the environment in which the child developed, rather than a hereditary or constitutional disposition. A child, who had to adapt to an external environment that was unable to assimilate his true self, would create a false self to cope socially, but this would deny his real self maturing.

Transitional object

One of Winnicott's most famous ideas is that of the transitional object. This object had to be chosen by the child and it represented the absent mother. He proposed that the object neither belonged to the child nor to the mother, but that somehow it represented to the child an intermediate thing that could bring comfort when mother was not available. It had a special significance to the child that could not be interpreted by anyone else. It could be loved and hated, cuddled and damaged; it did not get inside the child, but he attached himself to it for as long as he needed it. Then he could let it go, in his own time, without mourning it. It served to invest the world with meaning.

Potential space

This is described as the space between the carer and the baby, when mother is allowing the child some creativity of his own. It is shared between them, yet belongs to neither of them. The child can, in his fantasy, destroy or hurt objects, and yet they survive. Their survival is in no way generated by the child. His drive is to destroy that which he loves as well as hates. The object is able to withstand these fantasies and to continue to exist by its own capability. This enables him to learn of the permanence of objects; to then understand that his aggression and hate is not as destructive as he feared. It is important for him to realize that his love and his hate can be equally tolerated and the objects of his passions are not consumed.

Object relations theory

Winnicott had his own version of object relations theory. He spoke of the child perceiving two mothers – the object mother and the environment mother. The object mother provides the child's urgent needs, such as food and comfort; the environment mother manages the child's surroundings and interprets the world to him. As the child learns to tolerate both mothers, he is able to accept ambivalence. The anxiety about his strong instinctual drives needing to be vented on the object mother diminishes as he becomes able to make compensation to the environment mother. He goes on to accept his own aggressive tendencies as well as his loving aspects, neither of which has the capacity to annihilate his object.

Play

Winnicott had a lot to say about play. He felt it was central in the child's search for himself and throughout life; creativity has to begin with play. He felt that if a child could be absorbed in play, then he would be able to focus on things later in life. A child can only play when he can trust the environment and know that it is safe for him to become involved in his game, as someone will care for his outer environment. As the child develops his own play, he gives meanings to his imaginative ideas and feelings. Winnicott believed this was the beginning of cultural experience. He saw the risky nature of play, in that the child's imagination could run away with him, causing anxiety. However, it is possible for the child's anxiety to escalate to the point of the child frightening himself. Play then has to stop in order for the child to enlist the help of a carer who can hold the anxiety, by gently reassuring the child that in his external reality, the creations of his imagination are not a threat, but recognizing that the creation was a worthy endeavour. Winnicott also said that play was therapy in itself as it required that the child was totally honest and open in his interaction with the external objects that he had endowed with his own meanings.

Adolescence

The Oedipus complex as presented by Freud was challenged by Winnicott. He believed that in adolescence a young person needed, figuratively, to kill off both his parents in order to find his own identity. With the new-found power available to him, the adolescent has not necessarily achieved self-confidence to deal with his aggressive and sexual intensity.

Criticisms of Winnicott

There were several criticisms of Winnicott and it was a long time before he was accepted in psychoanalytic circles. He was criticized particularly for the emphasis he placed on the role of the biological mother and the absence of the role of father in his framework. He idealized motherhood, and some critics felt that he ignored the subject of infantile sexuality. Other examples of criticisms are that he tended to be over-optimistic about the negative feelings of the child; he postulated that the child uses a series of illusions to meet new situations; that he suggested that therapy could be a corrective emotional experience.

Primary needs

There is an emotional cost in working with the child's primary needs, as the child's emotions will be primitive. It is as the therapist and the child develop their relationship that the therapist can receive the transference communications of feeling and the child experience a different way of being heard. (Transference will be described in Chapter 3.) There is the possibility of experimenting with new ways of being and entering into a new constellation of connecting with other persons.

The counsellor can be helped by the theories of human development, particularly in the emotional domain. By referring to a framework, she can identify where the child may be struggling and what the relationship between herself and the child needs to redress. The building of trust is always the first step and the counsellor will be careful in setting the limits around the sessions. Those children who cannot trust must be understood and their anger tolerated. But the counsellor must not collude with the child by giving in to all the child's demands. These ways of working replicate the very primitive feelings of the child towards the main carer and the counsellor has to allow trust to develop and then allow the child to experience frustration, so that he can discover that it can be tolerated. When a child is struggling with trying to find autonomy, he may present as incapable of making choices, reject any help and show explosive behaviour. The therapist needs to help the child to make choices and to encourage the child not to give away the opportunity to choose. This may mean limiting the choices, so that the child does not have too many options that will make choosing more frightening. The young person who presents as having difficulty in managing any relationships with members of the opposite sex, and is jealous and competitive about everything has probably not managed the Oedipal conflict well, where longing for the attention and love of one parent has made him want to get rid of any other competing person. The counsellor will need to be careful to offer warmth which cannot be misinterpreted and to make sure that there is open discussion about any competitiveness, rather than collusion.

So to be aware of the general emotional development of children is essential. To then glean particular information about the child client's past can help a great deal, although the counsellor may not be in a position to have all the details she would like. But it is the meeting of the therapist and the child that has the greatest influence on the possible changes that can take place.

> We engage in a therapeutic process with the child which we know from experience can lead to greater emotional health and which will at times focus on particular areas of vulnerability as they arise in the child's material. But we cannot accurately predict what the outcome will be. Often, while making some headway in the problem that prompted the child's referral ... there are lateral shoots of growth which are quite unexpected and yet are indicative of increased emotional well-being and creativity.[19]

Summary

1. We discussed children's emotional development, using Erik Erikson's framework.
2. We contrasted the healthy outcomes for emotional growth with the difficulties that children and young people encounter when their needs have not been met.
3. Object relations theory is an important concept in working with children; and we explored some ideas from John Bowlby and Donald Winnicott.

4. Theories are helpful to the therapist as a backdrop, but it is in the personal relating of therapist and child that the work can go forward.
5. Children's early experiences set patterns for the future and, where their primary needs have not been met, the therapist makes opportunities for reworking and re-evaluating the meeting of these needs.

3

PSYCHODYNAMIC UNDERSTANDING OF CHILDREN'S PROBLEMS

Overview

Children frequently find difficulty in putting their feelings into words. Often they have not developed the vocabulary that they would need, but their feelings are very much a driving force within them. They feel passionately and either act out the feelings or turn them in on themselves, and communication between therapist and child can be used as a channel for the feelings. The important thing is for the child to feel that somebody is there to receive his message. He does not need it interpreted, but held. Sharing the feeling until its meaning becomes clearer helps the child to face it, rather than dismiss it.

Psychodynamic counselling

All psychodynamic work stems from the work of Freud, though there have been many other students of Freud's work who have taken his ideas into different directions. But that is what Freud would have wanted. He did not believe that he had found answers, but that he was raising questions about the mind. Ever since, people have been studying the ways in which personality develops and what constitutes the mind of a person.

Psychodynamic theory accepts that the unconscious part of the mind is available to hold memories that are not readily accessible to the person. This enables the conscious mind to function without too much threat to existence. The psychodynamic therapist will examine various dilemmas that children may confront in the light of how the unconscious may manifest its pain through behaviours that seem inconsistent with the conscious situation.

'Psychodynamic' relates to the vigorous interplay between states of mind. The child comes into contact with others and memory plays its part in depositing expectations of human behaviour. Present and future interactions will be coloured by past experience. The conscious mind will regulate involvement by acting on previous information, while those experiences which have been too difficult to process will lie in the unconscious, triggered at times by a connecting threat, when the child will react as though the threat were in the present. The child's internal world and the external world can be difficult to differentiate. Children become confused about time and the therapist should always receive information with caution, paying more attention to the child's perception and feelings around an event, rather than assuming the story as factual evidence. Staying with the child's reality is the better place, rather than casting adult interpretations.

CASE EXAMPLE

Catherine

Catherine was 3 years old and attending nursery. When her teacher asked if she had been given medicine before she came to school, she replied that she had. Indignantly, the head teacher telephoned her mother to ask why the nursery rules were being flouted. No child was permitted to attend if taking any medication. Catherine's mother assured the head teacher that Catherine had had no medicine that morning. She felt that the school did not really believe her, because the child's response had been definite.

It could have been that Catherine wanted to be mischievous on that occasion, or she may have thought there was some advantage to be had by saying she had been given medicine. Yet another possibility was that Catherine, at 3, was unable to distinguish that morning from mornings in the past when she had been given medicine. She had been asked if she had been given medicine. In her consciousness was triggered the memory of taking medicine and she replied that she had taken it. The head teacher had assumed that Catherine could think in adult terms.

Working with the unconscious

It is important that there is an understanding of the unconscious processes that are at work in all human interaction. In most situations, attention is not focused on these processes, but in psychodynamic therapy they form the basis of understanding the client's situation. If a child's behaviours are seen as just expressing what they feel at the present moment, there will be the assumption that the child is over-reacting to the current situation. If a child is hoping that the therapist will provide all that he requests, particularly in material things, then the child could be described as greedy. However, if account is taken of the child's primary needs that were never satisfactorily met by anyone, the child's greed becomes viewed through the eyes of need. A greedy child is not generally acceptable, but a needy child draws out sympathy and concern. Sympathy does not help the child. It is as though the adult looked at the child in a ditch and got down into the ditch with that child and stayed there with him. 'There is a term "empathy" ... which means ... that it is one thing to get into someone else's shoes, but quite another to understand what it is like for the other person in his shoes, while remaining in one's own.'[20]

The word 'empathy' is often used in counselling; empathy is seeing the child in the ditch and keeping one's own feet on sure ground, then reaching out and helping the child acknowledge he is in the ditch. The endeavour is to find ways of communication that will enable the child to climb out of the ditch on to steadier footing. But if the onlooker thinks that the child is greedy, the action taken would be to teach the child better ways. The therapist has to believe that the child is expressing real need and is crying out for some other way of being.

Children who have been hurt by life's experiences will not be helped by pushing them down further and telling them not to access their feelings. That would dismiss the feelings as of no importance. The child needs to find the reason for those feelings and to have someone who will listen to his story as it is expressed through play and talking.

Transference

The way in which the unconscious may be communicated to the therapist is through the transference. The therapist becomes aware of and pays attention to the feelings that the child is showing towards relating. She notes the way she feels about the interactions. This is not intrusive in the work, but is reflected upon after the session and in supervision. This is likely to replicate the relationships that the child has encountered before. It is as if the child brought into the session the contents from another place and tried to make them fit. His memory is in action. His internal schema is telling him that this new situation can be assumed to be like previous encounters and he will respond as though he were in that previous frame. None of this is put into conscious thought, but the child's ways of relating give the clues.

The therapist tries to piece together clues and to create an environment in which the child may be able to experiment with new ways of relating, as his anxieties subside.

Countertransference

There is also the countertransference – the feelings that the therapist experiences in being with the child. These feelings need to be examined in the light of the therapist's usual way of being. It is also important to distinguish whether there are other reasons for these feelings, rather than assuming that the child has been the cause of them. Examining the emotions and sensations raised is all part of the work and gives the therapist further insight into how the child functions.

Projection

It is an old aphorism that people criticize in others what they cannot see in themselves. Projecting into other persons the things that cannot be owned in oneself makes it easier to feel better about oneself. This is what happens collectively when there is an outcry against violence and a criminal is demonized. To lock away a symbol of violence is to feel it has been dealt with; then no longer does the rest of society have to feel that violence lies within and that every person has the potential to be as violent as to take life. It happens all the time. In counselling, children project bad things away from themselves. They sometimes cannot acknowledge their part, because to do so would be to become unacceptable in some way.

CASE EXAMPLE

David
David, aged 12, was a very distressed child. He attended a residential school and often became seized with uncontrollable rage. At lunch one day, David accidentally dropped cauliflower from a serving spoon on to the floor. He immediately accused the child sitting next to him of putting it on the floor. He became full of rage when the teacher explained how it had fallen off the spoon when David was holding it. It took some time to get David to look at the cauliflower and the spoon and to assure David that it could be picked up. He was not going to be punished in any way for what had happened. When David calmed down, he went through the situation again with his teacher, and for the first time in his treatment programme he took responsibility for his own action.

David had been punished severely in his early years. For him, the smallest misdemeanour had meant that he was banished to his room for hours on end. There he had wrecked his room in frenzy, desperate for contact with his mother. When he came to the school, he assumed that he would be treated in the same way. By this time, he anticipated punishment and could not believe that he would be accepted. His first reaction was to put the misdemeanour outside himself on to another child, hoping that he could preserve himself.

This is an exaggerated example of projection. Usually it is far more subtle. The person sees in others what he dreads most. The child who has had many placements that have broken down projects into his new carers all his fears of his being sent away again. Often this makes him test his carers to the limit. He cannot manage the fear of further rejection, so he interprets it as their fear of him.

Projective identification

In the above example, it is possible for the fear that the child has projected out to become a felt fear within the carers. They then feel that they cannot cope with the child and can be in danger of sending him away. When this occurs it is an introjection of the child's projection, and unless this is understood it can be internalized as a true feeling.

CASE EXAMPLE

Enid

When Enid was 14 she was told that she could have a dog. This was a longing that Enid had had for years. A care worker from the residential unit was to take Enid to a dogs' refuge. They were to travel some distance by car. Although the care worker was an experienced driver, she became very anxious about the vehicle she was to drive and began to feel that she might be exceeding her own capability. But then she thought about her nervousness and realized that she was introjecting Enid's anxieties. Having been let down by adult promises in the past, Enid was becoming more and more sure that she would not actually get her dog. In fact, when they drew up at the refuge, Enid breathed out as if she had been holding her breath for the entire journey. She gasped, 'I really didn't believe we would get here.'

The care worker had all the symptoms of the anxiety and felt the nervousness as though it belonged to her. Taking time to process what was happening enabled her to hold Enid's anxiety, but not to take it from her. Children need a place to deposit their high anxiety, but it must not penetrate the personal space of the worker. The personal space needs to be kept intact, whereas there is a professional space that has to be available.

Introjection

Introjection is quite a complex phenomenon. The projections from other people, who are getting rid of either good or bad parts of themselves as a defence, confirming their own ideas about who they are, are then taken in by the person on whom they have been projected, so that the recipient believes them to be part of himself. In the same way as the projector defends against owning the projected parts, so the recipient uses the projections in his own defence to confirm to himself his own perceived self.

Containment

The child who has not had enough containment and encouragement to know any kind of pattern in life is left feeling that anything could happen. Though this is partly true for every person, most people have had enough containment to know that though the unexpected can happen, for the most part life has regularity about it and can expect most of the day to go according to a plan. So what is this containment? Spurling writes:

> Together the finding of sanctuary and meaning constitutes an experience of containment ... .
>
> 'Containment' is ... used to describe an ordinary mental process whereby a disturbing experience can be made less disturbing by putting a boundary round it ... .
>
> In the therapy or counselling setting containment means the client has a powerful therapeutic experience of her frightening and intolerable feelings or thoughts being held and transformed by the counsellor and then returned in a digestible form.[21]

Containment is not about putting constraints on the child; the boundaries are put around the difficult thoughts and feelings. It is the therapist having the concern and emotional space for the child and his problems. It is not something that has to be forced into the mind, but it is being alongside the child in an empathic way that allows the flow of feelings to be shared. The child will then have found sanctuary and so be free to explore meaning with a person who cares. The setting up of rapport with any client is important, but with a child the place and the person have to be quite safe, for the child has to be sure that security will be available when meanings are sought, which may prove upsetting.

Privation and deprivation

The most difficult children with whom to set up a relationship are those who have experienced privation; that is, they have never been in a relationship that has been nurturing and containing. Therefore they feel that life is chaotic and makes no sense at all. Whereas an emotionally healthy child will have learnt some patterning in life's consistencies, the child who has had no consistencies cannot find any shape to form ideas about the external world. There are very few children who fall into this category, as even when a child has an inadequate or abusive relationship, there is the possibility of forming a pattern of bad objects. Though this is negative, it makes some sense. The child who has suffered severe deprivation or privation will not expect to find a caring adult in the therapist. On the contrary, his experience will have taught him never to rely on adults. So he may well try to sabotage the relationship by creating scenarios from his past which he knows alienate adults and draw negative responses. The more solidly his experiences have been confirmed, the more he will try to prove himself right and the testing will be more severe. He cannot dare to believe that this adult will be different. This is trying for the therapist, but she must persevere in reaching out to the client, even when the child is desperate to push her away. Barbara Dockar-Drysdale speaks of the feelings of annihilation that the child has experienced and of how he tries to make the therapist experience the same phenomenon. The child will project feelings of worthlessness and uselessness and only good supervision can give the containment that the therapist needs, putting the boundaries around the work that enable the counsellor to explore the process of what is happening. Dockar-Drysdale wrote:

> the experience of 'annihilation', which is so primitively destructive that one cannot talk about anything as personal as hate in this connection, and must be endured if treatment is to succeed. The child simply 'wipes out' the therapist; the therapist has to *feel* wiped out, rather than defend himself against the child.[22]

Winnicott spoke of the way in which mothers usually develop 'a state of heightened sensitivity' when they know they are pregnant and that this state continues into the first few weeks of the baby's life. He used the term 'primary maternal preoccupation' for this state and believed that the child was contained by the mother's focus on the child. Where this has not occurred, the therapist has to re-create for the child the caring adult who will be preoccupied with the child's needs. The therapeutic hour becomes the womb-like space in which the child can create the therapist, annihilate her, but then re-create her again, adjusting the creation to new information. The therapist thus becomes what the child needs on each occasion. She does not change in herself, but in the child's illusory world, he can be contained by his own projection of his needs.

Dockar-Drysdale wrote about 'archipelago' children who have 'islets of ego growth in a chaotic sea of unintegration'. The islets are formed from small good experiences, but overall are awash in a sea of unpredictability.[23] The task of the counsellor with these children is to help the child join up some of the experiences, so allowing a more integrated understanding to develop rather than a fragmented existence.

Stigma

Children who feel stigmatized for any reason find themselves outside what they believe to be 'normal'. It can be the colour of their skin, wearing spectacles, being physically challenged, sexuality issues, or having been abused. It may be something that is, in fact, accepted by others, but the child within himself is unable to come to terms with his predicament. The child will believe that the therapist is able to see the difficulty at a glance; it is as though the child had a notice across his forehead announcing his problem. Many adults may have rebuffed the child as having silly notions about himself. This will have compounded the issue and made the child feel alone with his problem, but also feeling foolish for having feelings which distress him. The task of the therapist is to allow the child's feelings and to accept that they are what they are, without criticism and with genuine understanding. The child needs to know that the therapist is listening to him and his story in a way that makes him feel he has a need that is not generalized to all children with the same need, but that he is unique and his needs are inimitable. The counsellor can have no role unless she perceives the child as the distinctive character he is and can identify with the way in which the child comprehends his situation. It is not making meaning from the therapist's stance, but helping the child to communicate *his* meaning.

Anger

Anger is a justifiable reaction to being treated unjustly. It is a healthy emotion; an emotion without which there would be no response to unmitigated violence, abuse or neglect. It is only when people feel anger that they are motivated to use the energy created by anger in creative ways to bring about positive change. Most of the reformers were angered by what they saw as injustice towards certain groups of people and resolved to make changes for the better. Freud described the structure of the mind as having three parts – the id, the ego and the super-ego. The first of these consists of the raw, primitive, natural instincts; the third part listens to expectations from the external world, and the ego is the developing self that brings under control the id as well as moderating the demands of the super-ego. The Freudian idea was that anger was bubbling away in the id and that it would try to overwhelm the ego. Neuroscience is beginning to show that anger does not have a life of its own. Hunger and sexual arousal are geared towards survival, the former to preserve present life and the latter to create new generations. Anger is also associated with survival; it arises when a person is threatened and gives rise to the fight-or-flight response. But anger is not necessary to survival unless there is a threat. There are plenty of threats that attack throughout life and small children are most vulnerable. This is because they are unable to make a considered judgement about a threat. Adults are more able to weigh up what the threat means and what choices of action are available to them. The threat does not have to be real; perceived threats are every bit as powerful to arouse anger mechanisms. Where children do not have the language to put their anger into words they can only act it out. If they are able to process the reason for the anger, they may or may not be able to direct their anger to the place or person of the threat. However, quite often it is impossible for them to make sense of its origin. The reactionary anger is all too powerful to be kept under control by the ego. It has to be put outside the conscious self in order to preserve the person. This anger erupts from the unconscious and is diffuse; when children first come into therapy often their anger is disseminated in all directions; everything is wrong and the therapist will be one more person in whom anger can be deposited. The expectation of the child will be that the therapist will reject the anger and with it the child, replicating his previous experience. The task of the therapist is to hold the anger, showing that the child can also be held. Margaret Hunter described her work with an adolescent who had been bullied; she saw her task as helping him 'distinguish between angry feelings which cannot be helped and aggressive actions which can be controlled'.[24] It is important that the therapist keeps the anger alive. Children who lose their anger have usually reached the point of despair. Anger offers hope that something can be done, that life does not always have to stay the way it is at present. Justice is still possible.

Courage is a characteristic that is valued in society; anger is often associated with courage. When a child or young person is angry, he can often find the will to confront difficult situations. Intellectualizing and denying anger are ways of turning the anger in on the self and then assuming that the things that aroused the anger have been deserved. But the situation then remains static. Anger needs to be recognized and acknowledged in order for it to become a vital force in making changes.

> People who have been wounded, victimized, and oppressed often repress or suppress both the event and the attending anger, which can lead to dissociation. Persons who have been through trauma early in life, such as in incest situations, and are left unable to communicate their fear and anger for fear of retaliation or rejection may have learned not to allow the anger to occur at conscious levels. The most intense way this separation occurs is through repression, the psychological term that describes what happens when a person's conscious process does not allow itself to be aware of something. A different level of response is when a person becomes aware of anger and it is immediately pushed out of awareness, dismissed from conscious concern – a process called suppression. Anger, then, can be lost as an expression of selfhood through either repression or suppression. In either case, the person's voice is lost.[25]

Depression, suicide and self-harm

Depression in children has often been doubted in the past; however, in the more recent literature, examples are cited of children who have suffered depression, often without introductory remarks as to whether this has been diagnosed accurately.

In 2002, the National Institute for Clinical Excellence in the UK was asked to give a clinical guideline for the management of depression in children and young people. This suggests that the problem of depression in children and adolescents is now recognized and being addressed to some degree. The rising suicide rate among young people, particularly young men, gives further evidence that depression is very real.[26] Linked with suicidal ideation and events are the many ways in which young people self-harm, including eating disorders. All these dilemmas become more powerful in the adolescent, as he tries to negotiate a path from childhood to adulthood. There are many pitfalls along the way. If parents hold too much anxiety about their child, the young person builds up more tension about how to disengage from the childlike state. There can be hopelessness about managing the task, which leads to depression. There may be a determination to keep control as one's own prerogative. Where parental control overwhelms the young person's internal control, eating disorders may ensue. The child and mother are closely associated in feeding all through life until adolescence. To refuse food is to create anxiety in the parent which can be an attempt by the adolescent to make the parent feel the angst that is pervading the young person's world. This is not usually a conscious desire, but a way in which the unconscious can play out in action the feelings of wanting to take charge of one's own life. At the end of the day, the child is the creation of the mother and father; there is no more dramatic way to hurt the creators than to harm or destroy what they created. Parents have a need to be vigilant, but they cannot go on living their children's lives for them. There comes a time when they have to stand back. This is not easy when parents are feeling their own decline in physical powers. There is unconscious jealousy in seeing children develop new skills, prowess and sexuality, but allowing the adolescent enough room to mature is pivotal.

CASE EXAMPLE

Graham

Graham was 15; it was his mother who contacted a counsellor for help for her son. He was displaying signs of anorexia. The counsellor asked whether Graham wanted some help and he duly attended several sessions. Graham described how his mother was exceedingly anxious about his eating. He found this puzzling, as his mother refused to eat normal meals at all. She was constantly telling him how she had let him and his sisters down by being such a bad mother. His father had been a depressive for some years and featured little in Graham's life. Whenever Graham wanted to choose an activity for himself, his mother would tell him that he should be doing something else. He should not go out with his friends because he needed to study. On one occasion, it had been agreed that Graham was to go to a music gig with his friends; as his father was driving him to the venue, his mother began to shed tears about her worries. Graham then capitulated and said that he would not go, owing to his mother's anxieties. If Graham challenged his mother in any way, she became deeply upset and hurt. Graham then surrendered as it made him feel guilty to see his mother upset.

The counsellor was able to help Graham to see that his mother was refusing to allow any movement towards Graham's maturity. She wanted to keep him within her framework. His father was not setting a model for his son of any other way of being. It appeared to the counsellor that the family was blackmailed by mother's emotionality. It was the mother who needed help for her eating disorder that was being played out by her son. Graham soon understood that he was in control of his eating and that he could use food refusal to make his mother stay outside himself. But he was in danger of identifying with her (or maybe she with him) and so perpetuating the closeness rather than confronting it. This was a real dilemma for Graham.

Niki Parker writes:

Infected by the heady brew of adolescence present in the family, parents may start to act out their unresolved adolescent issues alongside or in rivalry with their children ... .

In addition, socially adolescence is the time to join with the group and obey group mores rather than parental rules. This commonly leads to conflict between parents and offspring about friends, time to come home, money, clothes, how to wear hair, when and where to pierce ears – and other places on the body, sexual behaviour and relationships, issues to do with drugs – legal and illegal. If the family is not a safe place for all these conflicts and heated debates because it is not safe to express anger for all kinds of reasons, it might be easier to retreat to an earlier stage of development and get the issues addressed in terms of a younger child ... .

... What is remarkable in the eating disordered adolescent is how she has managed to be treated as a baby in making her parents worried about her food intake, whilst announcing at the top of her voice that she is fine and wants to be left alone ... Stern (1988) develops this concept by stating that it is not only 'refuelling' that is taking place; he argues that the child and parent need to share a *new* experience. Is this a clue as to what is being reworked with these eating disorders in adolescence where such intense attention has to be paid to the young person's feeding relationship – attention of the kind that would ordinarily only take place in the intensity of the mother–infant feeding relationship, and during the common conflicts over food that take place during the toddler stage?[27]

The therapist's role in helping a young person facing these dilemmas is to keep hope alive. This is not a hope that can be given to the client, but it must remain a belief of the therapist. If the therapist cannot visualize a future story for the young person, it is likely that the therapist will be pulled into the hopelessness felt by the adolescent. She needs to acknowledge the young person's feelings of hopelessness and stay with them, while maintaining the hope that the young person will come through to a new future expectation for himself. Young people will expect adults to behave in very similar ways to the other adults they have encountered. For those who have come to the point of feeling there is no future worth living, they need a new experience that will give them a sense of somebody who is listening and taking seriously what they are saying, trying to understand how their relationships are shaped. How the young person relates in the counselling session will give clues about this.

CASE EXAMPLE

Sandra

Sandra was in her mid-teens when she felt she could not cope with life. She was admitted to a psychiatric hospital and treated with medication. She became stable enough to transfer to a therapeutic community where she lived for two years. There she was offered therapy over an extended period of time. There were many times when she felt suicidal and she frequently described how she would carry through her intention; this brought her attention from other residents. Feeling very hopeless, one day she sat on the edge of the platform at the local railway station, thinking about jumping in front of a train. There she thought about the fact that she would be talking to her therapist that afternoon and she would be able to take her agony somewhere. She got up and returned to the house. It was a turning point in her treatment. She felt that there was one person who would listen and understand and that meant that life could be faced.

The therapist had not communicated her hopefulness to Sandra, but had held it when Sandra had no hope of her own. It was a long time before Sandra left the therapeutic community and lived in her own accommodation. But with support, she began to enjoy her new life in the city.

Sickness, disability and death

Working with children who are sick or disabled presents distinctive problems, yet emotionally such children have the same needs as their able peers. It is emotionally draining to work with children whose lives are likely to be short. It is also very depleting to work with children who are violent and disruptive. These children need and deserve therapy. There are all kinds of special provisions that need to be addressed, but above all the therapist needs to assess how she will manage the work and what support is in place for her. There is little use in agreeing to take on a child client with whom the work cannot be maintained. The treatment must never be thought of as a cure and there are occasions when there will be deterioration in the child. This has its effects upon the counsellor as well as the child and needs to be acknowledged. There are also dilemmas where parents do not want the child to know the truth about his illness and the counsellor cannot be as honest with the child as the child and she would wish. This is bound to put an artificial barrier in the room in the sessions, but it is not the counsellor's task to reverse the parental choices, no matter how much she may disagree with them.

There is a tendency for the counsellor to see a child with a disability in the reverse perspective, that is, to see the impairment and its effect on the child. This needs to be addressed; the more experience the counsellor has of working with children who suffer various disabilities, the more she will be able to relate to each child as a child with a disadvantage rather than a disadvantaged child. It is all too easy to think that the child's needs refer mainly to having to deal with disability. But the truth is that we are all disabled in different ways and each child needs to be seen as a new client with a different constellation of needs. In counselling, it is the emotional needs that have to be addressed with exactly the same openness as with any other child. The preparation that a counsellor makes to allow for physical differences and different levels of understanding should enable the counsellor to meet any child with a ready mind.

Working with children who have experienced the death of a parent or sibling is difficult; there are exceptional difficulties to be faced where the family member died a violent death by suicide, manslaughter, murder or accident. Where there has been illness, there has been some warning and often preparation for the event, but for the child bereaved by a sudden tragedy, there is the shock as well as the grief of loss. There is also the added complication that the other caring adults will have suffered the same shock and may be so preoccupied with their own grief that they are unable to give the child the emotional attention necessary. The counsellor needs to allow the child to address the issues without restricting the child's grief, enquiry or guilt. Being able to stay with the whole spectrum of emotions enables the child to feel safe in those expressions and will help the child to hope that he might one day be able to manage and toler-ate the awful feelings himself. Trying to alleviate the pain will only exacerbate the child's anxiety and may delay the grief process. If the pain he is feeling is toned down by others, the child will feel that he is not helping the situation and may numb his emotions, creating a hardened shell around himself for protection.

Abuse

Children who have been abused tend to be seen by counsellors as cases that bring with them a weight of anxiety for the worker. The truth of the matter is that the anxiety is already within the counsellor. People get anxious and want to relay the responsibility of abuse, reporting to a higher authority in order to be free from any accountability.

CASE EXAMPLE

Alan

Alan was a counsellor working in residential care. On one occasion a young boy drew some pictures, which could have been interpreted as sexual. They could also have been interpreted in many other ways. Alan's anxiety was high; he suggested to his supervisor that he should contact the child's mother. The supervisor wondered why this was Alan's response. Alan knew that cases of sexual abuse could lead to court proceedings and he did not want to have to give evidence.

The supervisor explained that there was no disclosure by the child at this time and the sexual interpretation was purely Alan's hypothesis. But Alan could not stay with this and sought out his manager, who assured him that there was no need for any action with the present information. But Alan persisted; he called in a senior manager who allowed him to report the child's possible sexualized drawing to social services. At this stage, the Social Services pointed out that the drawings gave no evidence to suggest that they should be concerned.

Alan's actions were fed by his own anxiety. He thus acted prematurely and no doubt his anxiety was apparent to his young client. If the child had drawn a picture and his counsellor could not contain it, how could he give the counsellor anything more? Although no progress was made, Alan's anxiety subsided because he felt that he no longer held the responsibility. Of course, action needs to be taken when appropriate, but the counsellor needs to be able to be with the child until he is able to communicate the most difficult feelings, and may disclose sexual abuse. There can be an excitement about sexual abuse that fails to take account of the emotional abuse that has accompanied it. Emotional abuse leaves deep scars and the counsellor needs to address the child's feelings as well as the events. To become fearful from a tentative remark or drawing suggests that the counsellor has an agenda of her own that needs to be addressed outside the client's time and space.

The transference relationship in the counselling is a significant feature of the work in psychodynamic counselling, as described earlier. Every detail of what happens in a session needs to be considered and reflected upon. The counsellor needs to be thinking what meaning the child's play and behaviour is showing. A student, when discussing transference, enquired: 'So if the child is telling me her cat is constipated, I might think she is holding something back?' Humorous, but it is considering material in that way, questioning all the time the message that the child is giving. It is not spoken about directly most of the time. The counsellor stays with the child's perceptions and images.

CASE EXAMPLE

Wendy

Wendy, aged 7, acted out how she, as a baby, kept crying. Her Daddy got so cross with her that he threw her out of the window. Wendy talked about how dangerous it was for the baby to be living with Daddy.

The counsellor was not alarmed by this fact, but understood that Wendy had picked up from her father that he wanted to be rid of her. It was her way of communicating what it felt like for her. The perception of the child is what gives meaning to the event; the counsellor journeys with the child through the meanings, to find more fulfilling ways of expressing the core self that needs to flourish. Many experiences may have restricted the emotional growth or damaged the struggling, tender seedling, but the life potential is there and the counsellor can sometimes see the buds developing. The child moves on before the blossoms appear, for they belong to the child and his future.

Children, and particularly adolescents, get caught up in family friction. Even when the difficulties between people in the home are not enacted in front of the children they can easily pick up the tensions. When children and adolescents do not know what is going on, they tend to create their own fantasies, which can terrify them. The therapist has to hear the dilemmas faced by the child or young person and work with their perception of the situation. There is no point in chasing the truth of the matter, but how the young person is affected is the presenting need. The young person may experience the tug-of-war in love and loyalty between the parents. There may be the feeding of information from one partner about the other. The therapist aims to help the child to establish and to validate his own feelings. We look at the home situation of the young person in more detail in Chapter 9.

Summary

1. Working with the unconscious aspects of children requires careful reflection on all the details of an interaction, but particularly with the feelings that are aroused both in the child and the counsellor.
2. We looked at the unconscious processes that drive children's behaviours, both positive and negative, in the light of psychodynamic concepts.
3. We sampled some of the events that may bring children into the counselling setting.

4

PLAY THERAPY

Overview

We all play and go on playing throughout life. Play has a special significance for young children who are able to rehearse real-life situations without incurring the consequences that would follow on in real-life situations. Children do not need toys to be able to play; almost anything can be used in the service of setting up scenes in which the child can make his own story. In therapy, play is frequently the main vehicle for communication, especially when the child is very young or too traumatized to speak about painful events.

The importance of play

Now I shall discuss an important feature of playing. This is that in playing, the child or adult is free to be creative. (Winnicott)[28]

Play is of vital importance in the development of children. The importance of play lies in the fact that it is the child's natural experience. He plays with everything that is available; play offers the greatest potential for learning. The child finds his thumb and plays as he sucks it, discovering comfort and a replacement for the satisfaction of feeding, when feeding is unavailable. He finds fingers and toes and plays with them, discovering that they belong to him. There is a wonderful world of discovery going on all the time for children. They need to feel safe to play, unhampered by instructions or an imposed adult view.

Babies respond to their mothers and the feedback offered to babies allows them to get an impression of who they are and how they are accepted or rejected in the world. In Chapter 2 we explored in more depth the infant/mother dyad and how the child interacts with his main caregiver, gradually learning not only to respond but to initiate activity. This relational aspect of early play is important. Later, the child develops play in a solitary way, enabling him to tolerate the times when the caregiver is away. Play can comfort, play can fill time with meaning, and it makes sense of being.

Play is a natural expression throughout life. The work of Piontelli showed that before birth babies in the womb play. Her remarkable pioneering work with ultrasound scans demonstrated that twins interact with one another in a playful way, but not necessarily in a loving way. She was able to show that the twins who cared for each other before birth continued to show care for each other after birth and the twins who appeared to fight with each other carried on in the same way as they grew as toddlers.[29]

Play is demeaned by the use of such phrases as 'child's play' to denote a task that should be very easy for the person concerned to accomplish. As Winnicott implied, play is not only the preoccupation of children, for we all go on to play for the rest of our lives.

CASE EXAMPLE

Stuart

Stuart, an adult client who had experienced the most appalling childhood, was the eldest of five children. He had been made to look after his siblings when he himself was a young child. The children had lived with their parents in a small tied cottage where there was no bathroom. The crux of his story was the fact of the 'shit bucket' being underneath his bunk bed, so that he could take it to any one of his siblings during the night as required. As he told this story and that of the later years, when he had fought so hard to train as a doctor so that he could get out of the poverty trap, it became obvious that he had been deprived of play. He could not remember any toys and Christmas had been a time when his father disappeared from the house in order to drink. This meant that he came home the worse for wear and knocked his wife about. The children were always very scared. Stuart had felt responsible for the younger children and had taken them out of the way into the bedroom. But there was no diversion for them; they listened huddled together in the corner of the room. They heard their mother crying out and the brutal threats of their father. After training as a doctor, the client recognized the importance of play and longed for some excuse to make up for his lost childhood years. When he married, he married a passive wife over whom he felt he had control.

This bears out the psychodynamic principle of the early attachment to primary caregivers laying down the blueprint for the child's future relationships. Choosing a partner is one of the most important relationships and it is therefore likely that in this choice the internal-izing of the parents' model of relating would be of huge significance. Bartholomew, Henderson and Dutton said:

> a family history characterised by various forms of inconsistent and rejecting caregiving would be expected to give rise to less secure models. Through an active process of construction, these insecure models would tend to lead individuals to recreate insecure patterns in their adult relationships.[30]

When Stuart had children of his own, he wanted to change the patterns from his own upbringing. When his own children were very small he insisted on giving them every play opportunity imaginable. But he could not let *them* play freely; he had to tell them all the wonderful things they could do. *His* need to play was interfering with the freedom necessary for his children to play. When the therapist suggested that he could have his own play time, he thought that the suggestion was wonderful, but could not allow himself such 'childish pleasure'. Play was for children, not for responsible adults. The therapist's suggestion was an unconscious mirroring of what the client was doing with his children. She was now suggesting what the client might do. The tragedy was that his play needs had never been met when he was a child, so now he was fulfilling his need through his children and thus depriving them of real creativity in their play. Play was so structured to be productive that there was no room for their own feelings to be played out.

Developing play

From solitary play, the child moves to parallel play, allowing others to play alongside, but playing independently of the other. During this phase, children can be very possessive of their own toys and look unkindly on anyone who might want to share. Play is focused on the objects, which have particular significance, and to take them away is to take from the child a part of the inner world of imagination and story. The child sees his toys as an extension of himself, much as he could not distinguish in his early infancy that his mother's breast belonged to a separate person and not to him. This is often referred to as the 'part-object', a term used by Melanie Klein. The child has blurred boundaries and needs to progress to reach a point of individuation, knowing what is 'me and what is not-me', a term coined by Winnicott.

However, it is not long before the child engages in co-operative play, when he wants to share the story with other participants. It opens out a whole new world of being able to have another with whom to enjoy experiences, with whom to laugh and with whom to cry.

As soon as rules come into play, there is a different dynamic at work. Rules mean that there is an imposition on play. Games and sports develop, which are good for all the reasons that co-operative play is good, but there is a difference in that the child *must* keep the rules or a penalty will be incurred.

Play may turn into a game, but it is only play for the child who is working out his inner world and making the story. For the other people involved in the play, it has become a game in which they are being requested to fulfil roles that have been assigned by a group member external to the other participants' own ideas. Even if a child can choose a role from a selection of parts, the creator of the story will decide the cast. This is why children so often walk away. Each child has his own story to fulfil and the child's story may be at variance with the other. Protest from both sides then occurs, for each child needs the other players to perform the other roles. This battle for trying to manage two worlds – the external and the internal – requires a degree of sophistication to resolve.

As the child matures, he changes the toys, gathering the things that make most sense to him. Some children want cars and diggers and love to see real-life roads and building sites. Others want dolls and brooms and like to help around the house. There is no fixed path for a child to take in the choice of toys, but of course there is conditioning in the external environment that impinges upon the child's selection. If there is a do-it-yourself person in the household, the child is likely to want a carpentry set; where there is a new baby, then dolls might well be popular; but the adult expectations of what a child might like also plays its part in shaping the child's interests by the materials provided.

The vestiges of solitary play can be seen in the popular activity of collecting various objects. Stamps, postcards, matchbooks, coins, keys, phonecards, beanie toys, etc., become possessions of the owners, yet allow for comparison and swapping between friends, but the collection belongs only to the child.

Adults continue to play in different ways. It is the medium that changes. The young child uses toys, which are representations of the outer world's existence, yet he is able also to use them for an expression of the inner world. Adults have their own playthings, but do not call them toys, except for the few executive toys labelled as such. Adults have golf clubs and sewing machines, tools and creative pastimes. These things are used in the same way as the child's toys. When a player hits a golf ball, how many times is the ball representative of a person, a feeling or a difficult situation upon which the player wishes to vent some inner feeling of anger or displeasure? The employee may not hit his boss, but the golf ball can be a way of releasing the tension that has built up in that relationship. Is this so very different from the child who wants to kill the tiger that is so threatening? Not a real tiger, but the tiger he imagines the mother to be when she will not allow the child to forget a misdemeanour.

Play bringing together internal and external worlds

The child has an inner world which he inhabits; he is often willing to share some of that world with others. He plays with his own thoughts and ideas, as he finds new ways of expressing things to himself. He then tries out his ideas in playfulness.

CASE EXAMPLE

Naomi
Naomi was 3 years old and attending nursery school. One of her new friends was a little girl who was a vegetarian. Naomi took in this information. At the weekend, Naomi's mother asked her if she would like chicken for her lunch and Naomi agreed. But by lunchtime, Naomi had changed her mind, and when her mother put chicken on the table, Naomi declared: 'I cannot have chicken, because I am a vegetarian.'

Naomi was trying out an idea that had been going through her mind. Her friend at nursery was able to have a different meal from the usual and so Naomi wanted to try it out for herself. She was playing.

External reality is the world in which the child lives with all its complexities. It is difficult to describe external reality, as reality is more about what the individual perceives than about the facts of any situation. Therefore there is no absolute for anything. There are no sure signposts to the way to adulthood. Every child has to find a way to get there, with little if anything of a recognizable route.

CASE EXAMPLE

Delia
Delia was 8 years old and was seeing a counsellor. She came back after a summer holiday and told her counsellor about a visit to Turkey. The highlight of the holiday for Delia had been when she had gone to the sands

and seen the newly-born turtles struggling to find their way to the sea. The parents had gone on ahead and each little turtle had to find its own way.

Delia was, in the same way, trying to find her way to acceptance within her family, her external world. Her parents seemed to expect Delia to be able to communicate with them at an adult level and were pushing her to be more mature than she could be.

Play bridges two worlds – it is neither internal nor external, but it borrows from both. Inner feelings can be lived out with the use of symbols of the external world. Toys become the medium for external expression of inner feelings and thoughts.

One of the most exciting ideas that Winnicott proposed was the 'potential space' (mentioned in Chapter 2), the area that develops between mother and baby as she adapts to his need to be more autonomous and she, in his eyes, regains an identity of her own. In therapy, this space also occurs, for the child client cannot remain dependent on the therapist. 'In other words, the mother's or therapist's love does not only mean meeting dependency needs, but it comes to mean affording the opportunity for this baby or this patient to move from dependence to autonomy.'[31]

Play is that which is both inside and outside, both objective and subjective. It comes from both mother and child and meets at a point where both can make use of it. It is a space for growth that can be used as desired.

The child is looking all the time for clues as to how to be. He looks to the adults and older children in his household for clues as to what is accepted and what is not within the domestic scene. For children who experience consistency within this frame, there is the opportunity to make some sense of the situation. Where there is inconsistency, the child is making a desperate attempt to work out any pattern or frame for behaviour. The world of school and the outside world are even more problematic where they set different codes of conduct from the home. However, what the child learns at home will have the most influence on how the child develops a set of values. Though these standards may be tested by other competing ideals, the child will be shaped most by the principles given at home; the principles children internalize are those lived out rather than the ones talked about. Children *do* live what they learn. But they learn what they see in action. Emotionally children need to see adults who can be trusted, who are reliable, and who can provide security and refuge. Adults can only provide for their children when their own provision has been satisfactory. This might have been their own early experience or a reworked compensatory encounter. Children also need the respect of those adults, knowing they are valued for who they are. With this self-esteem, they can interact with other children and adults with empathy and feel part of their world. Without the security, the respect and acknowledgement of them as valuable people, children will doubt themselves and be afraid of entering into dialogue with other children, other adults and the world at large.

Symbols are very important in the development of the child. The child chooses to represent his inner world by objects that stand for other people or feelings. It is very important that a therapist working with a child does not point out to the child that she knows whom or what the objects represent. This would make the child draw back from giving the story. As long as the object is not the reality figure, there is safety. As soon as the person represented becomes present in the therapy, it will no longer be safe. It is safe for Snow White to have a wicked stepmother, but it is not safe for the child to have any evil in his own mother, as this would be to destroy her. The therapist will not reach the hidden meanings unless she can stay with the child's symbols.

The value that is given to play in the child's external world will shape the child's ideas about play and his contribution to the social scene. If the significant people in a child's life enjoy play with the child, becoming involved in a lively way when invited and delighting in being left outside the play when asked, then the child will look upon his play activity as having value in the wider world. A child will soon internalize the message if parents use play as a means of keeping the child out of the way in order that adult activities may be resumed. The child will adopt the belief that play has a function for the adult, but no meaning for the interaction between them. Play is then relegated to a futile pastime and has no meaning in the world of relationships. As play is an extension of the child's ideas, he is diminished as a person not coming up to the required standards, if play is not shared in a meaningful way.

Why do children so often prefer the cardboard boxes to the toys that are housed within? It is commonplace that children play with wrappings more than with the toys, until encouraged to get rid of the wrappings. Could it be that the wrappings are part of the adult world as well as his world? The toys have no place in the grown-up world. Children love to play with things that are meaningful. Part of the meaning is apparent when they have seen others using them. Then there are attempts by parents to make sure that the child uses the toy as they would wish or as the manufacturer advertised, rather than allowing the child to use it for his own purposes.

CASE EXAMPLE

Maurice

When Maurice was very young, he used his food imaginatively. A pie would be a treasure chest that he would open, depositing his peas inside for jewels. His father was anxious that he should 'just eat his dinner', but his mother was keen to hear the story that Maurice had begun.

Adult expedience can dam up the creative expression of the child's play that can take place with any object. Maurice, in the example above, went on to develop his creativity and excelled in his chosen career. An early school report described him as having 'an intellectual curiosity'. He developed the capacity to think and work in innovative ways. Did this begin when he was in his high chair?

When Maurice had a daughter of his own, who put a carrot cube beside her dinner plate, put a pea on the carrot and a flake of salmon on top, making a 'man with a hat', Maurice imitated his own father, by telling his daughter to get on with her dinner! He was reminded about the opportunity given to him to experiment and how he had slipped into the adult way of seeing the world because he was the parent.

CASE EXAMPLE

Olivia

Olivia was the second child in the family. Her mother was quite controlling and rigid in her attitudes. She scolded the child often and, just before Olivia's brother was born, stopped breast-feeding Olivia to prepare for the new baby. The new baby was a boy and Andrew was favoured above Olivia. When Olivia went to playgroup, she held back. Both children were encouraged to achieve goals in their play and produce outcomes from their play, rather than using their own imaginative inspiration. But when she went to school and the school referred her for counselling, because of her anxiety levels, Olivia suddenly found she was encouraged when she was adventurous and developed her own ideas. She revelled in creating her own adventures, devising plans to go to the forest to catch tigers and find monkeys. She loved the worlds inhabited by the spectacular: space, the underwater world, volcanoes and dinosaurs. When Olivia discovered that the counsellor was happy to join in the play, she invented new episodes each week. Her mother found her exhausting and preferred Andrew, who was less tiring.

Olivia was asked to help with the baby and was rebuked firmly when she did not want to assist.

The weekly counselling hour gave Olivia the space she needed to help her play as the 4-year-old. There Olivia could let her imaginative play have free rein within a secure setting. At home, Olivia's activities were stifled by strict parameters. When she went to school, Olivia delighted her teachers and she was able to use the new school environment to gain in confidence.

Children can find that in different settings they are able to use play in different ways, but one of the most powerful tools for their future lives is their imagination. Where this is allowed to blossom, many of the difficulties in life can be played out, so rendering it unnecessary to act out in real-life situations the frustrations and anger that are part of a child's maturing self.

A child is not just the product of an environment, who can be taught how to be a human self. He is not a blank slate on which society can inscribe its own particulars. We now know that neural pathways are formed as the child experiences an ever-increasing variety of feelings and events. The unborn child has many encounters in the womb; its first kicking movements are perceived by its mother and the mother's reactions impart something to the child. Nearly every expectant mother talks to her child and imputes meaning to the child's movements, thoughts and future intentions. There is something within the newborn baby that is more than just a reflecting back of the feelings of the mother, though these are important. The child is a separate being as far as the mother is concerned. Mothers generally relate to their children from before birth. Relationship is not possible unless there is a separate identity. Mothers testify to the fact that each of their children, though reared very similarly, has his own individual characteristics. The way the child's inner life develops depends on good-enough continuous care; each child will experience his own way of relating to the mother. Because of the dynamic interrelatedness between mother and baby, no relationship can be replicated. It is in the inner world that the child develops a pattern of relating and feelings of selfhood. The external world brings much to bear on the child. The culture of the home, the locality, the social interactions of parents, and later, school and communities all help in the shaping of the personality. There are two worlds, the internal and the external, and the child has to live in both and somehow integrate the two. Unintegrated children cannot make sense of such an integration and cannot manage their own inner selves in conflict with the external world. A child may withdraw from the external and manage only the internal, using panic as a defence against the external world. Other children can manage the external world by denying their inner selves and creating a false caretaker self. The child appears to cope, but where the inner anguish is not addressed and an emptiness or compliance to the outer world ensues, there is an inner vacuum.

CASE EXAMPLE

Iona

Iona was 12 when she joined a group of children in residential care. She could not contain her behaviour at certain times of the day. There were two separate hours in the day when Iona would be restless. All the staff found her difficult to reach at these times. She would get toy cars and crash them together, getting extremely angry and tearful. Over a period of time, the therapist working with her was able to discover that the toy car represented real cars. Iona had formed a relationship with her class teacher and she was caught in a frenzy of anxiety that this relationship would be spoiled in some way. She eventually was able to say that she was afraid that the teacher would have an accident on the way to or from school. Her high levels of anxiety did not allow her to think about this possibility at first. All she could do was use the symbolic crashes.

As the work progressed, Iona was able to talk about her feelings of having killed off a number of people who had been close to her. Her experiences of having been bereaved had never been addressed.

Two years later, Iona was writing about a car that went off the road and was sinking to the bottom of a pond. There was no hope for the car and it would just rust away.

In the first use of the cars, Iona was giving clear symbols of the teacher's car. In the second use, she was representing how she felt about her own life. Sometimes symbols are more obvious than at other times. The child can deal with issues through the symbolism: it has similarities to telling dreams. In dreams, the unconscious becomes partially available for thought and consideration. Often there is not a full understanding of the dream, but there are some aspects that can give insight. The therapist works all the time looking for clues and helping the child to discover for himself the meaning of these shreds of information about the inner world.

Adult interventions in play

Play needs to come from the child's inner self and not be shaped to conform to external constraints. When a child is guided by another person in play, the direction comes from an exterior locus of control. Although the child may not resent this, the child is basically conforming to the agenda of the other person. To some extent, this has to happen in children's lives from before they are born, when they are totally dependent on the mother to carry them about wherever she chooses; to accept the food she chooses to eat; to imbibe any other substances the mother may choose to use. As mentioned earlier, mothers believed that they could transmit their thoughts and perceptions to their unborn offspring.[32] Neurobiological research shows that the neural pathways in the brain are affected by and linked with emotional and perceptual messages.[33] As the child grows, he is necessarily shaped into the norms of society; otherwise the child could not live as a social being in an external world. But play needs to have the quality of drawing from the child the precious parts of himself that lie within and come from his inner being with all its innate and original thinking. The young child has no words into which to put these thoughts until language is acquired. But language is not the only form of communication. Winnicott wrote:

> it is play that is universal, and that belongs to health; playing facilitates growth and therefore health; playing leads into group relationships; playing can be a form of communication in psychotherapy; and, lastly, psychoanalysis has been developed as a highly specialized form of playing in the service of communication with oneself and others. (original emphasis)[34]

Play, above all, is the space where learning takes place at the child's pace, with the child's agenda. It is the space that is allowed for the child to deal with inner issues that he has no means of expressing through the demands of others. Play has to be from the child's internal locus of control. It is the world in which he lives, that part of himself that is incommunicable to others in its complete form, for it is the very essence of what makes the child the unique individual he is. As Winnicott put it:

> I suggest that in health there is a core to the personality ... this core never communicates with the world of perceived objects, and that the individual person knows that it must never be communicated with or influenced by external reality.[35]

The adult as observer

Observing children's play may appear to the uninitiated as a simple pursuit. However, to make sense of, or to stay with the non-sense one can experience requires a great deal of concentration and a clear mind. It depends on the adult's role as to how the adult views the play. It is easy enough for a group of parents to be chatting together at a playground and to describe themselves as 'watching' their children. True, they will be aware if a child gets into difficulties; they will sometimes be addressed by their children to watch some feat of competence; they might remember the enjoyment of the child and the interaction of the child with other children. But the parents' minds in this situation are also open to other things – to each others' comments about the children or about general conversation. They may pass on local gossip or compare school reports. Almost any subject can be legitimately deliberated upon.

However, when an adult engages in a therapeutic relationship with the child, there is a different watchfulness. The adult has to have a completely clear space for the child. At each meeting the space must be there so that the child can use the space for his own purpose. Although the counsellor will not forget the information gathered from previous sessions, the child can start from any point at each new session. Adults tend to pick up themes, or leave the counsellor at the end of a session with suggestions as to what will be taken further in the next session. Children are very different; they have shorter concentration spans and may flit from one thing to another. What seemed to be of utmost importance in the last session may be completely absent in the next. It is a very important principle to remember that the counsellor's curiosity about previous material must not be allowed to intrude in a new encounter.

CASE EXAMPLE

Nigel

Nigel was 10 when he was referred for special help by his school. His teacher reported that in story time, Nigel sat at the back of the class masturbating. The other children ignored Nigel to a great extent and the teacher was at a loss as to how to integrate him. When allowed to use art materials, Nigel poured all the paints into one pot and stirred the mixture around vigorously. He then lashed paint in all directions, covering everything and everyone in sight.

When Nigel attended a therapy assessment, he moved all the furniture in the room to one place, trapping himself in; he then proceeded to dash madly from one activity to another behind his barrier. The session was full of activity, but no clear meanings were evident.

The therapist watched Nigel intently as he charged around the room. She was aware of the anxiety building up in herself, as she tried to absorb the feeling of the frenzy from which Nigel could not disentangle himself.

To keep up with this hyperactivity and have any sense of what is happening is extremely difficult. To have any other thought in the counsellor's mind is impossible. In calmer sessions, often the child is not telling the therapist what is happening, but is acting out the feelings through play. The child's state of mind can sometimes be seen in the activity levels of play.

Feelings that cannot be spoken can be played out in the security of the counselling room.

After many sessions of the frenzied activity being accepted, Nigel gradually began to show a less turbulent pattern in his play. He was able to reach the deep feelings of sadness that his hyperactivity had masked for a long time.

CASE EXAMPLE

John

John was a boy whose mother had died as a result of taking an overdose with alcohol. John had seen his mother drunk so many times that he did not realize his mother was lying on the floor dead when he came home from school. He did nothing for a while, expecting his mother to get up at some point. When it was time for his tea, John tried to rouse his mother, only to be confronted with a 'brown' face. He then grasped that something was very wrong; he ran into a neighbour and implored her to come with him; an ambulance was called and the child was told his mother was dead. A wrangle broke out between relatives as to who should have the care of John. He attended counselling and played with teddy bears who visited the 'house of death'. The counsellor had to act the part of the witch who came and stole away the bigger teddy. John did not talk about his mother, but it was obvious from his play that the matter was prominent in his feelings. He showed his anger for the witch, but also for the teddy for going away.

In playing the assigned role with John, the counsellor was able to experience and accept the anger that the little teddy felt, knowing that these were John's feelings, but accepting them in John's way of relating.

The counsellor has to be with the child, looking on, but also entering the child's inner space, to make meaning from the activities and to pick up and contain the feelings that the child wants to have contained, until the child is ready to take back into his internal world the feelings that have been processed, made bearable and can then be owned.

The invitation of the child to enter a new world

Entering the child's world is not to see the child's world through adult eyes, but to experience it through the child's perspective. This can be difficult where adults have any residue of their own childhood knowingly or unknowingly unresolved. It is of the utmost importance for counsellors to have their own therapy before embarking on counselling children. There will be times when the counsellor will need to engage in further therapy because unconscious issues begin to surface in the light of a child's pain. There are two dangers here; first that the counsellor wants to work with children to work through problems of her own without realising what is happening; secondly that the counsellor may have resolved some problems of her own and therefore think that the resolution lies in a specified answer. These dangers can be more likely when working with adolescents because the counsellor usually remembers more about the adolescent years than earlier childhood. A counsellor may have children of the same age as those coming for counselling and may feel that she is a good parent and therefore able to use the same kind of reasoning with a child or adolescent client as with her own offspring. But no two children are the same and to assume any way forward is to put an adult perspective on the child's world. The counsellor may be a good parent, but parenting uses different skills and a different relationship from the counselling alliance.

It is useful for trainee children's counsellors to try out a physical exercise to underline this point.

EXERCISE

Sit or kneel on the floor to make yourself the same height as a child would be. Look at the world and other people from that point. Realize how high up everything appears to be and how difficult it is to engage in the normal way. You see people's waistlines rather than their faces; you see the dado round the room rather than the pictures on the wall. Other people tend to be looking over your head and not engaging with you as they engage with one another.

In the physical world, this is what a child experiences. But in the emotional world, there are parallel differences between adult and child. The child's mind has only a small amount of the knowledge that the adult has accumulated; there are so many things that cannot be understood and have no meaning, because the child's experiences have not expanded as yet. The child sees a part of things, but cannot comprehend the whole. There are adults who talk about faraway stuff and use a vocabulary that is vast and unintelligible. Yet there are snippets that are fathomable. The danger is that the adult assumes that the child's world is a foretaste of his own extensive knowledge and so can be subsumed into the same body of learning. But each individual has a different path to take and the future way is always unknown.

CASE EXAMPLE

Denise

Denise, an only child, was referred to a counsellor by her parents when she was 9 years old because both they and Denise's teacher had concerns that Denise lacked confidence with her peers.

When Denise first saw a counsellor, her father intimated that the playroom was certainly not the place where Denise should have her therapy. She needed the room used by the older children. The counsellor gave the child the choice of rooms and explained that if the child wanted to change rooms at any time, she could do so. Denise immediately chose the older children's room, but within three sessions had asked to go to the playroom, where she made very good use of the facilities.

Denise's parents were high-fliers in their careers and they had assumed that Denise would be more adult than her years. At home, they did not make allowances for her age, as they assumed that Denise was a bright child who could engage in adult conversation. They were interpreting her world as they saw it, not as she saw it. They were pulling her ahead of her years and emotional maturity and wanted her to work at their prescribed pace. Denise needed the space to play as a younger child and find acceptance at a level of play that was her own expression of herself.

The counsellor has no right of access into the child's world, no matter how much she may desire to get alongside the client. It is only through trust that the child will allow the counsellor a right of passage, and it may take a very long time. With young children, there is often the opportunity to engage in long-term play therapy. With adolescents, it is often not possible to create the transference relationship. Teenagers feel that they need help, but they want it for a specific discrete unit of behavioural change. They want to get the show on the road again, to be back with their mates and not engaged in a lengthy consideration of what is happening for them. This may be a defence, but often a necessary one, amid all the turbulence of their struggle to become independent without necessarily having the skills to manage it adequately. It is a time of being suspended between childhood and adulthood, swinging from childish dependence to mature independence. During this phase, the idea of playing, even with ideas, may pose a threat. Although vacillating between childish and adult feelings, the therapist needs to be aware that she might be construed as the opponent rather than a mate. It is unlikely that the young person will want an allegiance with an adult, and he will certainly not want to think of his therapy as play. It is not in the interests of anyone to assume that a long piece of work will be more advantageous. This is not always the case; there are adolescents who want to go more deeply into their past history and to use the therapeutic container in a more profound way, but others are too fragile to work in depth. To trust can feel like conflict with the adolescent's bid for independence, the need to create a space between himself and the parent figures.[36] To engage with a substitute adult could cause more resentment.

But with child or adolescent, trust is not automatic by any means. Children and young people come for counselling because all is not well. Most clients come because they have had difficult experiences that have not been processed. Often the feelings they have been left with are those of mistrust; the adult world feels far removed and adults have frequently let them down. Trust is not necessarily in their emotional vocabulary, and where there has been inadequate encounter with significant persons in the child's past, the counsellor will have to be prepared to be treated in the transference in the same way as those who have let the child down. This can be difficult for the counsellor. She wants to give the child something new, but the child cannot reach out for it. The counsellor has to receive all that the child gives, whether negative or positive. The young child will communicate through play and requires the counsellor to either watch that play without suggestions or to be part of the play, always allowing the child to lead. The child's world is new to the adult in every way. It is not a real world, yet is the child's inner world being expressed through a third position.

CASE EXAMPLE

Paul and Harry

Paul and Harry were brothers whose parents had problems. The parents asked for counselling for the children, as Paul was making it difficult for the family to survive his obsessive behaviour. He wanted nobody to come into the family and no member of the family to go outside for any purpose. This was alarming the parents. Paul could not be persuaded to see the counsellor on his own, so it was agreed that the two children should be seen together. In the first session, Paul sat with crayons and paper as far away from the counsellor as possible. Harry was willing to move about the room and chatted informally. There were looks that passed between the brothers when Harry mentioned the family. For many weeks the pattern continued, during which time Harry described the mother in a family of dolls as 'Cruella'.

Paul described how they were shut in a cupboard when they had been naughty and how he felt that he needed to give Harry some hope and comfort. So he had devised a game in the cupboard. He pretended there was a window and each time they were put in the cupboard, he treated it as an opportunity to make up a new scene through the window. His favourite scene was where there was snow on the ground and he and Harry played snowballs and built a snowman. He felt all this had been very silly and was shy about admitting to this game.

It was obvious to the counsellor that the children were well aware of the hostilities going on between their parents and Paul's wanting to keep the family together without intrusion was a physical way of expressing his fear that the family could suffer a split. After a great deal of patience, the counsellor was let into Paul's world in a fascinating way. To be allowed into such a world was a great privilege for the counsellor. Such imaginative play had been the survival technique of this pair of little boys. Instead of focusing on the cruelty, they had found a way of transforming their punishment into a new and better world. It was outside themselves, yet they had internalized enough of something good to avoid being emotionally annihilated. Although their parents had ignored their existence when they were banished to the cupboard, they had stayed alive by being 'through the window'. All the worlds of children have pain as well as pleasure; the counsellor needs to appreciate both and to go into the child's world when invited.

There are many exciting adventures on which to go; adventures in which the child sometimes succeeds and sometimes fails. The adult needs to be the safe place from where the child can venture forth on his great exploits. There will be victories and defeats, heroism and cowardice, but the child who has built a trusting relationship will have a safe place in which to rehearse his achievements and his disappointments.

Playing different roles

The child may need the counsellor to play many different roles during the course of the counselling. As there are only two people in the room, all the characters need to be allocated between them. Often the child is acutely aware of the scenarios he wishes to act out. The counsellor is given roles as and when the child determines. There are, of course, limits to this. The counsellor cannot be drawn into a play role that would involve being abusive to the child in any way, no matter how demanding the child might be. The counsellor needs to think quickly as to what the role in the game will mean and how it will or will not serve the purpose of the therapeutic task.

CASE EXAMPLE

Joe

Joe was a small 12-year-old boy who suffered from asthma. He had been made fun of because of his inability to play football and keep up with his peers in sport. Joe's parents had split up three years before Joe attended counselling, and he had gone to live with his mother and brother. The home was quite neglectful and Joe did more or less what he pleased. His attendance at school was erratic and he visited his father on occasions. His father then remarried and he and his new wife had a baby of their own. One day, Joe's mother felt that Joe's behaviour was spiralling out of control and told Joe he must go and live with his father. She took Joe to his father's house and left him there. Joe's father was perplexed, but his new wife offered to try to help Joe and her parents were very supportive. Joe's bad behaviour, not surprisingly, continued to escalate.

In counselling sessions, Joe asked the counsellor to find him. He climbed into a cardboard box and said it was the only place he had to live. But the counsellor was a kind lady who came to look for him. She took him to her home and looked after him. This drama was re-enacted many times. Further on in the counselling, Joe asked the counsellor to be a policeman and arrest him for having drugs, but the policeman was asked to beat Joe and manhandle him. The counsellor refused this role, much to Joe's disgust. He insisted it was only a game, but the counsellor could see that Joe was trying to make her another abusive adult. After talking with Joe about his feelings, about how people did things to him and how helpless he felt, Joe talked about his older brother and the humiliations he had suffered at his hands.

In this case, the counsellor had to decide that the role of the policeman and an arrest for drugs was appropriate, but abusive behaviour by the policeman was not acceptable. Joe wanted to bring the counsellor in line with his previous experiences of adults. To use the policeman was subtle, not a direct request, but the counsellor needed to be aware of how the child would be able to confirm his view of adults as abusive if she acted out the role.

CASE EXAMPLE

Isabel

Isabel was 7 when she started counselling. In her early life, she had been rejected by her mother. She was a foster child in a family with several foster children, among whom were her two younger sisters. Isabel immediately trusted the counsellor, to the point that the counsellor was worried that the child might become too easily attached to any adult. Because of her past history, the counsellor also felt that the child might only be able to hold on to shallow relationships. But the work went on for nearly two years. Isabel wanted to be the counsellor's baby and the counsellor had to look after her. Little by little, Isabel grew into the toddler, then into a schoolgirl, and then into a young lady who helped the mother.

Maybe the instant connection with the counsellor was the way in which Isabel managed to defend against the adult letting her down. She gave the impression of relating well, but it could have been a superficial false self that was presenting. The counsellor saw Isabel developing normal patterns of emotional growth. Isabel had a dread of the sessions not being confidential and of her foster parents being given information. There was some rigidity in the placement that allowed for little movement, but in the counselling room, Isabel had the freedom to grow herself, with an attentive adult looking on and providing for the child's developing emotional needs.

This play was appropriate and the child used the different stages of growing up to test out having a caring adult in settings from babyhood to adolescence. Hopefully, Isabel would look forward to a future in which adults could offer her care and allow her to become a part of a growing relationship.

Making meaning of play

When counsellors first begin work with children, they often find it difficult to make any sense of the meaning of the child's play. Some counsellors have worked professionally with children in different settings, e.g. social work, teaching or nursing. These professionals have an extra hurdle to overcome to work as children's counsellors. Teachers have been used to getting children to learn something from their activities. Play therapy is different. Children will learn a lot, but the counsellor will not have something in mind. It is true the materials made available will have an influence, but children are very able to give different meanings to the objects with which they play. A chair does not have to be used as a seat; it can be a cave, a ship or an island.

Adults do not like to not understand. They want to know what everything means. They feel they can only be with the child when they do not struggle to understand. The child does not understand a whole host of things and cannot make sense out of the experiences that are being showered on him. To not know, to not understand is to be standing with the child rather than in the adult place. That is where counsellors need to be. The counsellor has a dual role – to be in the child's place, but also to have the adult perspective when necessary for the child's safety and well-being. When the child cannot tolerate the not knowing, the counsellor can. The unthinkable anxiety of the child is thinkable for the adult, even though the counsellor empathizes with the child's position.

Interpretation

Having made some sense of some of the child's play, the counsellor can interpret what may be happening and what it is that the child may be expressing. However, the counsellor must remember that he is not the authority on what is happening and must not be tempted to give the explanation to the child. The interpretation can at best be a hypothesis with which to work. It can be useful for informing the counsellor, but the child is not to be informed prematurely. If the counsellor suggests that the child is expressing a particular emotion, the child must have the freedom to accept or reject the hypothesis. To suggest to the child that the emotion is the expression of a traumatic experience would put the child into a difficulty. Some young children want to please adults and would therefore agree with any suggestion of the counsellor. The danger is that the counsellor's hypothesis might be completely wrong; then the child would be led away from the internal world of his own into the world of the counsellor's projection.

CASE EXAMPLE

Molly
Molly was a counsellor working with a 5-year-old girl, whose mother asked for an appointment to discuss the child; she came accompanied by a neighbour. The neighbour explained that the mother was not very able to express the difficulties the child was having and proceeded to state that the mother suspected that her daughter was being sexually abused when visiting her father at weekends. The counsellor tried to get the mother to talk about her own perception of the problem, but she only stated that she agreed with her neighbour. The mother said that the child was not reluctant to go to see father, nor was there any sign of distress when the child returned.

The counsellor worked with the child for some time and, during the play sessions, the child showed that she was aware of intercourse by mating animals. Molly felt that this must have something to do with the visits her client made to her father. She discussed her hypothesis in supervision. The counsellor's supervisor constantly reminded the counsellor that she was interpreting the child's actions as demonstrating the mother's hypothesis. As yet the child had given no indication about any sexual interaction with her father. Eventually, the child disclosed that it was her uncle, her mother's brother, who had been sexually abusing the child and it came as a shock to Molly, who had taken on board the mother's and neighbour's suggested reason for the child's distress. By holding in her head an idea (that had come from outside the playroom), she was interpreting the play as supporting the hypothesis; this was interfering with accepting the child's storyline. Fortunately, the counsellor did not let the child know her thoughts and so the child came to her own disclosure. It could be that, if the counsellor's head space had been freer, the child could have disclosed sooner.

A child needs the counsellor to have the space for his own work. A clever counsellor who knows what is in the child's mind can be a frightening prospect. There are children who at an early age have switched off contact with parents, because they have feared that a parent could get inside their heads and know what was going on. When a child reaches a certain stage of development, it is necessary for him to be able to have a secret. To know something that is withheld from the caring adult is to have one's own identity. Two little girls once saw a dead cat in the gutter. They decided not to tell anyone about it – it was to be their secret and neither must tell. It took the form of 'we stared at a dead cat'. Both the girls kept this secret and often in later life reminded one another of their first secret. If the counsellor knows things about the child that the child has not given to the counsellor, things can become muddled.

CASE EXAMPLE

Thelma

Thelma was a very disturbed child, whose emotional experience had been horrendous. She had been the subject of sexual abuse and her parents made outrageous promises that were never fulfilled. As she was falteringly telling her teacher about some of the frightening things that had happened to her, the teacher listened. Gradually Thelma was able to give more information about a network of abusers. On one occasion, the teacher suggested to Thelma that she might be talking about something related to the abuse, when Thelma was relating details about her pet dog. In wide-eyed amazement, Thelma became highly excited and declared that the teacher could see what was going on in her head.

This was an untimely intervention. Though it was a correct interpretation, it gave the child an added anxiety – that the teacher had magical powers to get inside her. Thelma might easily have felt that this intrusion was similar to the abusive intrusions that had been made upon her in the past.

There are parents who wish to give information to the counsellor, which the counsellor would prefer not to know. It is good if the child knows what parents are saying. Some parents want to tell the counsellor about misdemeanours in the previous week. One counsellor asked parents only to say things in the presence of the child and not to telephone the counsellor prior to the child's session. The parents found this very difficult, but what they were trying to do was to influence the counsellor to work with their agenda rather than allowing her to work with the child's agenda.

Knowing is not the important thing; to be able to stay with the not knowing is more important. To be with the child where he is and to let the child work in a safe place at his own pace is what is required. The child needs to find his own interpretation. Winnicott said: 'the significant moment is that at which *the child surprises himself or herself*. It is not the moment of my clever interpretation that is significant.'[37]

Summary

1. We looked at the importance and value of play.
2. Children's contribution to the social scene through play communication gives a launch pad for them to feel valued.
3. In play, children can use objects from the external world to symbolize their internal feelings and perceptions of their circumstances.
4. Entering the child's world is a privilege which demands the therapist's respect.
5. Knowing when to interact and when to be the spectator requires wisdom.
6. The therapist may or may not make sense of children's play, but listening to children on all levels is more important than interpreting playroom happenings.
7. There are myriad ways of working with children in the counselling room and the next chapter outlines some of the ideas for play.

5

USING CREATIVE OPPORTUNITIES IN PLAY THERAPY

Overview

There are so many ways of using the limited time of a therapy session with a child. In this chapter we look at a few of the ideas that can be used. What is in the playroom is necessarily limited, but careful thought as to the ages of the children using the room can make the space comfortable, challenging and exciting. The therapist's own ideas will be better than ones that are second-hand, so the ideas here are not a definitive list, but a launch pad for the therapist to create her own original ways of working with play.

We looked at the importance of play in the previous chapter. Play encompasses so many activities, and this chapter focuses on the very practical ways of using different ideas in the therapy room.

Painting and drawing

Children begin to make representations on paper, chalkboards and sketch toys very early on. Making marks with paint, felt tips, crayons and chalks is one of the earliest attempts to create something. Marks on paper can be made from an early age and the child may describe what he has drawn, when the observer is unable to recognize shape or form. But there comes a time when the child begins representational drawing.

Figure 1 shows the drawings of a 3-year-old who has just made the transition to making distinctive animals – a leopard, with spots; a tiger, with stripes; a giraffe, with a long neck; and a snake. He declared that the symbols at the bottom were his name. Before this, his animals tended to be a body with four legs, but with no distinction between one animal and another.

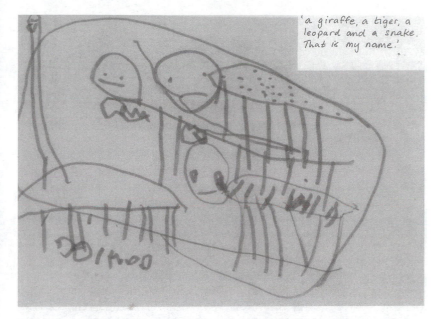

Figure 1 'a giraffe, a tiger, a leopard and a snake. That is my name'

The use of colour in artwork is of some interest to the counsellor. A child who uses bright colours is generally holding some positives about his experience, whereas the child who only uses black or pencil, when there is a wide variety of options, he is likely to be withdrawn and feeling quite negative. With older children, the formation of images and the way in which they are executed can give useful information to the counsellor.

Figure 2 was drawn by a 10-year-old who was very distressed at the time. It was one of a number of pieces of artwork drawn during his therapy. When a child attends counselling over a period of time, the progression in the child's drawings can be seen. They form a serial commentary on what has been engaged with during the sessions. Although the counsellor is providing the safe place and time for the client, the child may not, at first, be able to engage directly. Instead he often welcomes the opportunity to put his feelings 'out there'; that is he wants to engage with the counsellor but may not have words to express the inner feelings. Putting something outside the self so that it is available to both the self and the counsellor is to engage in an act of sharing.

The counsellor's role while the child is drawing is to share the emergent creation. If the child is talking as the picture develops, then

Figure 2 'a snake has come out of its hole. It is very angry'

the counsellor responds in a reflective way. If the child creates the picture with no comment at all, the counsellor should also be quiet. If it feels that there is no communication in the silence, the counsellor may comment on a factual basis. She does not need to comment on the images, but may comment on the colours used or that a part of the picture seems to be very special because the child is taking such a lot of time and care over it.

Some children may be very reluctant to put anything on paper. They may claim to be unable to draw. If this is just a matter of lack of confidence the child can be reassured that the counsellor is not wanting a work of art, but just something that the child wants to put on paper. If the child is struggling and is obviously devoid of any ideas, the counsellor might use Winnicott's squiggle technique[38] and put a squiggle on the paper for the child to make into something, or suggest that the child make a 'pattern'. This often frees the child to begin work by doing a repetitive, easy shape. This can give the confidence to proceed.

It is important that the counsellor should stay in the realm of the child's communication. This means that she will need to use the symbolic language that is offered by the child. If the picture shows a monster attacking a baby, then the counsellor talks about the monster and the baby rather than trying to get the child to talk about what or whom the monster might represent in the child's external life.

Where children begin to draw or paint is of interest. So, too, is what is in the foreground and what is in the background. What is in the picture? (It is easy to overlook some of the details.) What is not in the picture? The counsellor needs to think creatively about the underlying messages that she is being given by the child. Do faces have their features? The child who feels that he has no voice may well draw faces that lack mouths, whereas those with no eyes may be expressing things that the child would prefer not to see.

The study of the use of colour and the symbolic meanings of things drawn by children is fascinating, but it is not very rewarding for the counsellor. In fact, it can be positively dangerous. If she has in her mind that certain symbols have specific meanings, there is the temptation to interpret a child's drawings from the counsellor's mind. This is not a genuine understanding of the child. There are no universal symbols. It is the child's meaning for his picture that has the significance. Although there is agreement from some writers on some symbols, the child's circumstances give myriad reasons why he might be drawing a symbol for a reason beyond the generally accepted meaning.

CASE EXAMPLE

Katie

In her early life, Katie had been sexually abused and had seen herself as bad. When she was 16, she drew a picture of a kitten on a tray; on another tray there was a big, black book. Katie could not make up her mind as to which of the two trays she wanted to have. She said she had to make a choice. Katie told the counsellor that kittens meant fun, they were playthings and mischievous. On the other hand, the big, black book was like a Bible, it was serious and very important. Katie's dilemma was that she felt that she had to choose either being serious or having fun. She could see no possibility of having both things in her life; she either had to dedicate herself to a serious 'calling' or she had to abandon serious life and go for the fun. The counsellor asked Katie whether the kitten and the book could possibly be on the same tray. Katie could not accept that possibility; the counsellor talked about the tray, which Katie described as being insecure and could be lifted and carried away too easily. She then worked through how the kitten and the book would be better if they had a more secure place.

According to some writers, the cat represents desire, liberty and stealth. If the counsellor had assumed any of those meanings, she would have missed the client's interpretation, which was very clear. For Katie, there was a split between the two; there could be no compromise. She was struggling to know how to look forward to a future in which she felt that she could not choose the serious or the fun without losing out. Ambivalence for Katie was no way out; she thought this meant that she was incapable of making choices. In doing this Katie was working through her own issues of being in temporary accommodation, where she felt she was being pressurized to choose a totally serious way of life – she even mentioned that perhaps becoming a nun would keep her in the serious state of mind she half-heartedly craved. But there was the other part of her that wanted to have fun. Her problem was that to have fun, Katie felt that she would have to let go of her serious side. To find a new place of safety meant finding a place where she could both have fun and be serious. But she began with the belief that such a place could not exist. It took a lot of work for Katie to integrate the separated parts of herself and to accept them both as valid. She had hung on to this image of herself because she could not bear to think of her dead father, her abuser, as anything other than good. Katie was an intelligent young person and was applying for a college course, when she felt that she could not carry on until she had worked through her anxieties.

If the counsellor had told Katie any of the ideas from others about her drawing, Katie may well have been lured into thinking that the counsellor must know and the richness of the client's own work might well have been missed. Or Katie might have lost trust in the counsellor, feeling that the counsellor would have nothing but her own ideas to offer.

Drama and role play

Children naturally express themselves by what they do. Play is a healthy way of learning about the world, but also about oneself. Drama in the therapy room takes many forms. The child client is always the instigator of the drama. It may be played out solely by the child, or the child may invite the therapist to play roles within the drama. The therapist needs to be able to enter into the drama without too much inhibition. At the same time, the therapist may be required to step back into her adult role to keep the client safe both physically and emotionally. There is a very telling piece of work described in John Allan's book *Inscapes of the Child's World*.[39] It describes how Luci, diagnosed as autistic, worked through the various stages of emotional growth to attain an integrated ego. Part of the work involved the therapists allowing Luci to dictate to them the roles they should play and accepting some difficult attacking behaviour from her. But there were times when they had to stop Luci and rescue her from her own destructive impulses, showing her the containment that she needed. Luci had inadequate internal containment and therefore the locus of the containment had to be from an external source. If the therapists had made no interventions, then Luci might well have felt that her attacking behaviour was spiralling out of control and that she was unable to contain herself. This would have been a frightening experience. The intervention meant that Luci knew she would be kept safe from destroying through her attacks. Quite often, a young person fears their own emotions and needs adult assurance that the adult can survive the hostility and violence.

Another theme that arises in dramatic activities with children is the role reversals that they initiate. This can be very therapeutic, particularly for children who feel that they have no control over their lives.

CASE EXAMPLE

Colin

Colin was 10 when he began his counselling sessions, which lasted for over a year. His mother had three boys, Colin being the eldest. Colin had been told by his mother that the man who was now her husband was not Colin's father and Colin had weekly contact with his natural father. Mother and stepfather were both suffering from chronic fatigue syndrome, which left Colin having to care for all the family at times. There was not much money in the home and Colin showed that he was well aware of this. He presented as a compliant child and trotted out many adult phrases of appreciation for his mother and why it was so much better for him to be with his stepfather than with his natural father.

In therapy, Colin began by taking the role of a poor peasant who was treated very harshly by the lord of the manor. The therapist was put into the brutal role and made to order the peasant to do menial tasks without giving any thanks at all. But later, Colin loved to take the domineering role and made the therapist the poor child who was not allowed to have any fun, who must work from morning till night. The therapist was told that the work was not good enough and there were always tasks that had not been fulfilled. Colin gained a sadistic pleasure from inflicting these burdens on the therapist, no doubt helping her to feel the pain of his home situation. But at the same time, he was working through feelings and trying out what it would be like to have power. At first, in the powerful role, Colin was as ruthless as he felt his demanding parents were on him, but gradually over time, he used the role to use his power in a different way. He became understanding of the therapist's dilemma and began to encourage rather than demand; he began to say that he understood. When he asked for the roles to be reversed back again, he was able to allow the therapist to be much more positive and gave her permission to say what she wanted to say. This enabled the therapist to address some of the feelings that Colin was dealing with and to talk about how things could change. Colin's school reported that there were differences in Colin's behaviour with the other children. At the beginning of the year, Colin had been hard on other children, had always wanted to be the dominant character in any game, and the other children had opted not to play with him because of his excessive demands. By the end of the year, Colin's teacher said Colin now had friends and he was much more amenable to playing with other children and joining in their games, rather than imposing his will on everybody else.

Colin's mother announced that she was expecting another baby. Although Colin spoke in adult terms of welcoming the baby, in his play, he was able to show the therapist that the forthcoming event would not be all that his words conveyed. He put himself in a house constructed by moving toys and furniture about the room; he curled up in a corner and complained that he had no room to move. The baby doll, on the other hand, had plenty of space. Colin complained that he could not sleep at night because the baby cried; he beat the baby in an attempt to stop it crying. Colin wanted to have a sister, as he already had two brothers, but he felt that the new arrival would cramp everybody. He talked of the suggestion that his parents had made that they could extend the house, but he was gloomy as he spoke of the poverty of his parents, who talked about good things happening, but the reality was that things could not happen without the financial resources. This enabled Colin to talk of the many times when he had been disappointed. Sometimes a teacher or a friend had promised things and they delivered on their promises, which made Colin realize more that his parents lived in a world of unrealistic hopes.

Colin was taking a more adult outlook than his parents. His home environment demanded this of him, but he was being robbed of his childhood. Therapy was the space where he could be the 10-year-old boy. His home situation needed to change and Colin's mother agreed to be counselled in regard to her negative feelings towards Colin. During the transition, Colin was able to enjoy the freedom of his play sessions as well as working on his issues. His therapy was his sanctuary in his busy, responsible week.

When writing about dramatherapy, Chesner has said: 'clients are invited to try things out in action in the therapeutic, dramatic space, where the context of illusion and play give permission for more freedom of exploration and expression'.[40]

All play is in a measure drama. The child knows that he is a person, but it is quite in order for him to become another person, animal or object and to behave as if he were that other. There is a suspension of reality for the time of play, but the child in no way believes the reality of the play situation. That is, the child does not confuse the play character with his own character. After the play, the child is able to return to his real person. At times, the child can go in and out of reality and fantasy, alternating between playing the assumed character and giving other children instructions or information in his real character.

CASE EXAMPLE

Giselle

A 14-year-old, Giselle, was recommended for counselling by her school. Teachers had noticed a difference in Giselle over the school year. At the beginning of the year, she had been a bright, bubbly student. But latterly Giselle had become withdrawn and quiet. Giselle found it difficult to talk to the counsellor and it was obvious that she felt ill at ease in the first session. Giselle did not want to use any of the art materials and said she wanted to talk, but did not know how to begin. The counsellor suggested that Giselle might choose an object to talk about to make things easier. Giselle then talked about a vase that was quite old-fashioned, that was on a table behind a door. When people came into the room they tended to push the door back on to the table. The vase was likely to be knocked off and broken. Giselle went on to tell how the vase was tired of having a dried flower arrangement in her. She wanted fresh pink carnations that filled the room with their scent. Then surely the owners of the house would move the vase and put it in the middle of the room.

This picture language enabled Giselle to express her feelings without any mention of herself. The counsellor worked with the vase and flower picture for a few weeks until Giselle made the links to her own life. She was feeling shut out of the family who had a new baby boy, who was receiving all the family's attention.

Puppets

Some children are unable to give voice directly to their experience, but they can be helped to show the counsellor their inner worlds by projecting their stories on to an external object. In this regard, the use of puppets can be instrumental in the child speaking through a third party.

CASE EXAMPLE

Polly

Polly was a traumatized 12-year-old and she acted out aggression and hostility towards anyone who approached her. She had very little interaction either at home or at school; the educational psychologist had diagnosed Polly as an elective mute. In the playroom, Polly loved the puppets and spent a great deal of time putting them in various parts of the room. She would then go to each one and smile at it. She was not using any verbal communication, yet she was showing an interest in having interaction by her smiles. She was guarding her fragile self but allowing contact by handling the puppets and showing pleasure in her smiling. Her counsellor worked with the puppets for several weeks, often pretending to listen to the puppets and conveying to Polly that they liked to see her smile and they wanted her to know that they liked to play with her. Soon Polly began to whisper to the puppets herself, but not in any way allowing the counsellor to overhear. Soon the puppets were used to whisper back to Polly. She would then look at the counsellor as if to want to include her. Gently the counsellor said that she wondered what the puppets were telling Polly. Very slowly, Polly began to say that the puppets knew what had happened to her. For a long time, Polly told the counsellor her story as though it had been given to her by the puppets. She worked at the feelings that sexual abuse had instilled in her, that she was not safe when anyone approached. She wanted to make friends with her peers, but dreaded trusting them in case they would prove to be betrayers of that trust.

The puppets were an intermediate stage for Polly and puppets can represent many of the significant people in a child's life. A good array of puppets is helpful; ordinary people-characters, witches, dragons, bees (for their sting), cuddly creatures, snakes, fierce animals, monsters and a number of other things can give the child access to act out many different emotions. Again, the therapist must allow the child to explain the choice; the general image of the fox is as a cunning schemer, but the child may have a different interpretation. This must be heeded. The child can use various puppets to work out conflict situations. The fights in which the puppets engage might be showing the tussle that is going on internally. The child has the opportunity to let a different character win on different occasions, thus testing out how it might feel if the conflict were resolved in one way or another. This is beneficial for the child. He may act out the same story time and again, but may vary the outcome, again trying on for size ways of getting through dilemmas. Where the child may have been the victim in a situation, he might give the character that represents him the power that was not available in the real situation. This gives the child a sense that power has not disappeared for ever, but that different outcomes can be attained. It is rehearsal for the real world conflicts that might occur in the future. To regain a sense of power is to take back into oneself the feelings that once were overwhelming, but might in the future be subdued, allowing the child a sense of freedom in his own abilities and strength. A child who has to fight in order to survive can learn how to sublimate that hostility into action that will be profitable. Often a child works from hostility to imagining the outcomes of the hostility and finding other ways to deal with the anger that is justifiably present. For many troubled children, there has been the expectation that they will have one specific role within the family setting and they have become compliant to that role. There is a rigidity that has not allowed them to express their own spontaneous selves. If they had dared to do such a thing, their existence within the family would have been threatened. Preserving that place has felt as though it was the only role for survival. The counsellor needs to be aware of this type of rigidity and allow the child to make small steps into the world of drama, using puppets or role-play scenarios. Making choices to respond differently might well feel like jeopardising the child's individuality. But with the support of the counsellor's presence, the child may venture to try out other ways of coping, especially if the trial can be made in another role. The child might also be able to encounter opposite feelings within play. He might be feeling as though he is at the bottom of the heap, yet in another characterization could play out feeling omnipotent, successful and powerful. To experience such feelings through playing out another role can lead to the child beginning to recognize new opportunities in the reality situation. This is movement towards reframing one's potential and allowing for new possibilities.

Puppets need to be plentiful; a puppet theatre is a luxury but a table and/or chairs can make ample performance areas.

Prose and poetry

Children love stories; stories describe the way of being and what life is like for themselves and for people outside themselves. The fairy story is a medium that touches each person's experience. They have survived the test of time, because they link into the feelings that every person encounters. They usually begin with the central character(s) being introduced, the scene set and a dilemma to be faced. As the story unfolds, difficulties and dangers are encountered, but through all the struggles, the hero or heroine comes through triumphant and life is changed from rags to riches, from despair to hope. So the child can believe in the promise of something better and hope enables the child to go on in the present struggle, in the anticipation that there is something that will change around the corner. Though things look bad, by twists and turns, by cleverness and cunning, there are ways through the thicket to the castle of dreams. Bruno Bettelheim's wonderful book about fairy tales[41] gives clear insight into the collective understanding of fairy tales and why they are different from other literature. The well-loved stories remain popular with children through generations and every culture has its own treasury of tales that are handed down to children. There was a move to take out all the frightening parts of stories, giving children a sanitized version of the tales, but these would not have given children the facility to deal with all the real feelings that arise within them of jealousy, despair and hatred. In stories they are able to identify with the characters and work out in fantasy what could not be tolerated in reality.

As well as fairy stories having significance for children, there are the stories that come from the child that give the counsellor insight into what is going on for the child in his inner world. There may be favourite stories that have a special meaning for the child and the child may want to retell the story or compose one that has elements of the original but with different characters or some different scenes within it. Such manipulations of the story should be encouraged; the child's adaptations are of importance to him and hold a rich reserve into which the child can allow the counsellor to search for meaning. Some stories are completely new and express so many feelings. Where a child can make up his own stories, encouragement needs to be given. Most of the time, children do not want to write down the material as that would be an onerous task. In this, the counsellor may ask if she could write the story for the child so that it does not get lost, or a tape-recorder may be used. Mostly, children enjoy the experience of listening to themselves telling the story. When they hear the recording, it can be edited. The material is then available to the counsellor in a form that is easy to access.

Some children have a natural gift for poetry, both in appreciating rhythm and metre in poetry of all kinds, and in creating their own rhymes or blank verse. A counsellor can learn much about a child who engages in reading and making poetry. To share the delight of words with a child is a very special experience. For a child who has a sense of literature, but has been undernourished in the beauty of language, the counselling session can become a place where the child finds joy in words and can use them to construct word pictures of what life is like for them.

CASE EXAMPLE

Felix

Felix was 8 years old. His parents were not very aware of their children's emotional needs and left them to their own devices for much of the time. With his teacher at school, Felix's class read the poem 'The Highwayman' by Alfred Noyes. The poem really kindled something in Felix and he wrote an amazing piece of prose of the love affair between the landlord's daughter and the highwayman. The head teacher read the piece in an open assembly and remarked on its exceptional quality. When Felix took it home, his mother put the piece of writing in the rubbish bin, saying that she had no use for it. When Felix attended counselling, it gave him a place where his poetic interests were accepted and shared. He was able to talk about how he felt that his family had no room for him or his abilities. Unless he emptied himself of his school success, he could not be accepted at home. This was a real dilemma for Felix. Should he pretend not to like his school work? Should he do badly at school, so that his parents would like him more? Over time, Felix was able to come to terms with his own strategy of working hard and enjoying his success at school, while not entering into arguments at home about his success. Felix's brother had often gone home and told his parents how Felix had been mentioned for his good work. This had then been ridiculed by the whole family. But by this time Felix's brother was at secondary school and so Felix was no longer subject to this ridicule for his success.

Felix's feelings for poetry and prose were very fragile. Nurtured, they would grow and develop into pleasure he could enjoy throughout life. He wanted to be assured that his delight in language was not showing that he was less acceptable as a person. The difficulty that some children face is that their abilities are not appreciated and they then do not continue working; they feel there is a choice between their talent and acceptance by their families.

Sand and water play

Sand is a material that can fascinate children and they seem to be keen to play with sand for many years. It is not only small children who get pleasure from sand, but older children also enjoy time with a sand tray in front of them. A child can create his world in the sand, using small toys. It is easy to bury things in sand and to put them out of sight with no trace. Discovering things in the sand can also be a pleasure.

CASE EXAMPLE

Kim

For weeks Kim played in the sand tray and hid crayons in the sand, wanting the counsellor to find them. Kim wanted the counsellor also to find the things buried in her life that were too difficult to find. She later asked the counsellor to hide the crayons, but wanted to be told where they were, so that she did not have the frustration of having to look without enjoying the instant gratification of finding. As time went on, Kim told the counsellor where to find the crayons she had hidden and then she opened up small parts of her story of abuse.

It can be quite frustrating to play the repetitive games children require, especially if the counsellor feels she is not getting through to a stage where she is doing the real work. However, it is necessary to go at the child's pace all the time, so that the child does not withdraw.

CASE EXAMPLE

Philip
Philip was 11 years old when his parents felt that they were unable to cope with his sexualized behaviour. He worked with the sand for many months. When he saw the dry sand he would put bucketfuls of water to saturate it. Then he submerged all the animals under the water. There was a lot of sexual activity among the animals. The male animals worked all the time and the female animals just sat around and they never looked after their young. Then there were massive scenes of violence and death. At one point, Philip held the therapist's hands under the water and asked her to keep them there.

Philip was showing how he felt about what was going on in his home. Philip's early life had been characterized by violence between his mother and father, which he had witnessed. Because it was too painful for him to contemplate, Philip had banished it from his conscious mind, but it was played out in his sand work. He knew that underneath his presenting life, there were many things that would be frightening to encounter, but with somebody there to keep him safe he could explore those hidden depths.

In the sand, children can erect barriers; so often they make enclosures to ward off things that would overwhelm them. There are spaces in which they can explore freedom to move. There can be conquests and submissions. Often children choose to line up the toy items so that there are warring parties and a conflict in which people get hurt and are often extinguished. Then there are reconciliations between those who have been waging war.

CASE EXAMPLE

Penny
Penny had soldiers on either side of a line she drew in the sand. All the little figures had weapons, which were other items. At first Penny overran all the

opposing forces, which were the counsellor's side. But gradually she would take some of the fighting and some of her soldiers would be killed. But finding no pleasure in this, Penny devised a game, in which the soldiers had to die, but after a certain amount of fighting, they could be recovered from the sand and they could stand to fight again. This was played over many times.

As Penny played out this scene, she was growing stronger in facing the challenges of her real life. There were conflicts that appeared to have no resolution at all at the beginning of therapy, but as she played her games, she also owned the possibility of reconciliations and of alternative ways of dealing with the issues she faced.

Water play is messy, but there are great advantages in having a water tray where space permits. Water gives pleasure and children are able to use water for dramatic rescue scenes. People easily drown, but they can cry out for help and then the emergency services come to the rescue. Small boats can give refuge from the storm, or they can capsize. Things can be thrown into the water and taken out of the water. There can be calm seas as well as the rough; the sea can yield its harvest as well as devastate the earth.

CASE EXAMPLE

Valerie

Valerie's father had died when she was 5. Three years later her mother felt that she had not come to terms with her father's death. Valerie attended therapy for nine months. In that time, Valerie began by showing how much she wanted to identify with her father. When playing with the water tray, Valerie put three figures in a boat. The larger figure fell out of the boat, and though he yelled for help, there was nobody to save him. Then the other two figures fell out of the boat; they yelled and one was saved, but the other did not want to be saved. This one wanted to go down in the sea where the other figure lay helpless. Later Valerie drew the water-tray enactment on paper and at the end of one session, she flew out of the door with the picture and showed it to her mother. On the picture, she had written 'He is dead.' The third figure was back in the boat, sailing along. When the counsellor picked up this story at the next session and the relevance of showing her mother, Valerie was deeply upset and said that she thought her mother had carried on just as though nothing had happened when her father died. She wanted to be sad about her father, but her mother could not cope with her sadness. This was a turning point in Valerie's therapy. She was able to talk to the therapist about her father and how much she missed him, how she had been to the funeral and visited his grave. But mother had kept father's car in the garage and said she could not part with it; all father's clothes were still in the house, and everywhere Valerie looked it was as though her father had not died.

In this example, Valerie had come to terms with her father's death, but her mother had not. Although the counsellor suggested that Valerie's mother might find counselling for herself helpful, she refused and said that she had been counselled at the time of her husband's death and there was no more to be done. She liked to live as though her husband were still there. Although the counsellor explained that Valerie and her younger sister needed to share their grief with her, Valerie's mother said that she could not bear to do it. Valerie stayed with her therapy until she was able to hold her own grief in a real way. The grief work had been delayed for three years, but Valerie was able to do this with the help of her therapist, as her mother was unavailable.

Playroom equipment

There are so many things that can be put into a playroom, but it is important that it does not give the impression of being cluttered. The choice of appropriate toys will be determined by the client group that is likely to use the room. If the same room has to be used for teenagers as well as younger children, it is important that toys for the younger group can be put out of sight while adolescents are there. This can be achieved by having lockable cupboards in the room. All age groups can make use of drawing materials, so these can be readily available.

If the counselling provision has the luxury of a dedicated children's room, where younger children can play, careful thought needs to be given as to what it should contain.

Dolls' houses are often given a prominent place, with families of dolls that can be used for many purposes. A very good idea, if possible, is to have two houses in the playroom. So many children spend time with separated parents; going from one house to another is part of their lives. To have two houses enables them to play out the differences and helps the counsellor to understand the feelings that are evoked by having two bases. Other children often use the second house for visiting other family members or friends.

Toy telephones are really useful, as a child may speak into the handset, although unable to have the direct conversation with the therapist. Children use telephones for emergency situations; they love to be able to call the doctor, the fire brigade or the police. Dialling '999' has excitement in itself and to be able to ring the number in play is to feel what it is like to be able to contact powerful people who can be called to the rescue. A sand tray is a very useful tool, but there needs to be a dry sand area as well as a wet sand tray. Otherwise, children who come into the room after another child may well find the sand under water and of no use for their play.

Almost anything can be helpful in the playroom. Narrow shelves within the child's reach can accommodate all kinds of small objects that can be collected from almost anywhere. Shells, jewellery, road signs, creatures, trees, animals, fences, fairies, witches, cars, aeroplanes, buses, trains, pretend food and puzzles can all lend themselves to being used by the child.

Of course, games and storybooks are other items of great value and there should always be the opportunity for some art and craft work. Art and craft materials are different from making a picture. The child has access to a plethora of materials and can use them just as he chooses. Creating models and making something out of mixed junk materials has for a long time given children enjoyment. With the counsellor, a child has an ally in trying to carry out a plan. There is often frustration at not being able to produce the finished article in one session. Paper, card, boxes, tubes, fabric and all kinds of other materials lend themselves to the child's imagination. There have to be adequate tools to enable the child to make what he wants. Hammer and nails can be there if wooden blocks are available. Scissors, glue and glitter are usually well used. Children need to be able to join things together and to cut things apart. In this way they are able to build and to demolish. Where there is no area for such activity, the child can use the many kinds of construction toys available. Lego, sticklebricks, Meccano and wooden blocks are all useful for the construction and demolishing of imaginary buildings or people. A child cannot get rid of certain things in reality, but with the toys he is able to knock down some of the things that seem to block his way forward.

Creative therapies can be used according to the therapist's choice. If a counsellor feels ill at ease with a particular way of relating, it is better not to offer the child that particular activity. Children are able to pick up the feelings in the room and it needs to be devoid of the counsellor's apprehensions.

CASE EXAMPLE

Pamela

Pamela was a therapist who could not bear wastage of materials. When her child client wanted to mix the paints together or combine play-doh colours, she warned him not to do it.

Pamela's anxiety about the cost of art materials was given priority over the child's need to express the messy parts of himself. Her communication to him was that the materials mattered more than what he was trying to convey to her.

It is perfectly acceptable to limit the materials made available in the room, but to make them available and not allow the child access, or to criticize his use of them is to tease him in a way that produces frustration rather than accomplishment.

Lighting and heating in the room need consideration; making the room as safe as possible is important. If there are clients who are likely to use objects aggressively, objects that could do any harm would be better out of the room for his sessions.

Summary

1. We explored various ways of working with children and made tentative suggestions for playroom equipment.
2. The space and the resources available will largely determine what equipment and facilities can be offered.
3. Children enjoy art and craft activities, drama and puppetry, stories, poetry and home corners, as well as sand and water.
4. Observing children's interaction with different materials and their communication (both verbal and non-verbal) with the therapist allows both to share experience.
5. Each child is unique and will bring a new set of relations to bear. In the next chapter we look at some special things that some children bring to the work.

6

WORKING WITH DIVERSITY

Overview

There is a whole range of differences that we can meet in children. Diversity in ability, family background, sexual orientation, ethnicity, disabilities, schooling and self-esteem will make every child client unique, so the counsellor needs to respect the child client and to work with issues that the child brings. There are various views on how closely therapists should be matched with their clients. What is most important is that the therapist is prepared for the client in a way that helps the child to know that he has been considered in an individual way. The child then recognizes that a space has been prepared for him and he will feel more comfortable in using it.

Difference

There are differences that have to be acknowledged. In the present climate of not labelling children, there can be a danger that rudimentary needs are not thought about. A child in a wheelchair needs the therapist to have thought about the access to the therapy room, its layout, the accessibility of play materials, the toilet arrangements, etc. Children with other difficulties need to know that their therapist has prepared for them to come. Every client needs to have that space in the mind of the therapist to feel valued. Each child will have specific needs and, where these demand alterations from the norm, arrangements must be carefully thought out *before* the child is offered an appointment. 'Otherwise, a patient knows he has not been thought about. The environment can be just as handicapping as the handicap.'[42]

Disabled children are likely to have experienced more physical frustration than their able-bodied peers. All children, in some aspect of their functioning – physical, mental or emotional – have been restricted by their circumstances. Special children often have impairments from birth, which means that they have, over time, perceived their difference from others. The question as to why they have been dealt a disadvantage can breed rage that is also not understood, which escalates as the child realizes more and more limitations. The therapist is likely to meet this primitive rage in the transference during therapy. It is difficult to work with distress in children at any level, but when children have so much of an extra burden in their lives it will not be an easy task to spend the counselling hour with such primitive feelings.

Diverse values

Every child counsellor has her own set of values. Those values have been absorbed, considered and revised throughout her lifetime. She has chosen to retain or discard the principles of those around her at various stages of her life. Training will have given the counsellor other values to think about and value judgements will have been discussed. It is not possible to counsel others without having a value base. The difficulty is that each client comes with a unique pattern of cherished principles and the more distant that pattern is from the pattern of the counsellor, the wider the gap that has to be bridged. When a child comes with a totally different set of values from that of the counsellor, acknowledgement of the difference is the first step. Counsellors like to feel that they will understand their clients, but a wise counsellor starts from the premise that she does *not* understand. In order for the counsellor to understand, the client has to explain. This is more difficult when the client is a child who is playing rather than an adult who is using the same language as the counsellor. The adult has usually forgotten the language of play and may have a tendency to want to interpret through her own mature thinking. Play has different interpretations; these belong to the individual child, who may or may not share meanings with the adult. Sometimes he will not recognize the meaning of his play, but in the playing he may gain relief. The counsellor must wait until more clarity is available.

CASE EXAMPLE

Miriam
Miriam, a bright 16-year-old girl, was finding it difficult to manage at home. Her father had remarried, which meant that she and her brother now had two more stepbrothers. Miriam's unhappiness was showing in her behaviour; she was moody and uncooperative at home and the sixth-form college she attended was frequently contacting her father and stepmother to

say that Miriam's work was deteriorating and they were concerned. The stepmother was a teacher and she had become distraught about Miriam's wasting her abilities.

In therapy, Miriam wanted to talk about how she felt that she had lost her father's attention; how she and her brother had become closer and were siding together against the rest of the family. Miriam was drinking a lot of alcohol with her friends and felt that young people should not have to fit in with adult expectations. She stated that the adult world had got it wrong; people should be allowed to do as they pleased. Work should be optional and the government should pay people to be unemployed if that was their desire. The therapist allowed Miriam to talk over a number of sessions about what she wanted for her life. She had ambition and could see that she was sabotaging her own expectations as well as those of her parents and the school. But she needed her own identity and she was afraid that if she identified with the reconstituted family, she would be losing a sense of her link with her mother who had died when she was a small child.

With the help of therapy, Miriam began to reshape her life, reframing her stepmother as an ally rather than a threat to her birth mother. She became much more a part of her family and her behaviours changed. Her school work became her passion and two years later she had gained high enough grades to take a place at her chosen university.

The therapist could so easily have put first in her mind the need for Miriam to change her behaviours. But already Miriam was receiving criticism and concern from home and school. The therapist's values were totally different from Miriam's stated values, but she received Miriam's ideas without criticism, entering into real discussion about the issues. In this way, Miriam felt affirmed and felt that she was being treated with respect and her views were being heard. This was a new experience of an adult who could challenge, but respect her. Her stepmother's anxiety was high and Miriam liked to see her suffering; she had not before understood how much she was harming her true ambitions by trying to let down the teacher part of her stepmother.

Diverse physical features

We all have differences in the way we look physically and the way we do things. Some of these differences are very minor, though a child client may have some minor issues that need addressing in therapy. For example, children who need to wear spectacles can sometimes be teased and bullied; left-handedness can make a child feel awkward and different. But there are also the bigger disparities that require more thought as to the suitability of the play area.

For the child who is physically challenged, there are different needs in the playroom. A child who uses a wheelchair will need access to materials that are displayed in a way that is reachable. A child who is deaf will need access to a counsellor skilled in sign language. The blind child will need a counsellor who is experienced in working with children who are blind and can provide play experience that helps to progress the work.

Each child who suffers from a challenging hindrance will have a special set of difficulties to overcome, but also a different set of attitudes towards the impairment. A child who has a positive attitude can devise his own answers to difficulties and will respond more to counselling than the child who wants other people to come up with solutions. Children with the same difficulties can approach them in different ways.

CASE EXAMPLE

Tina and Moti
Tina had a rare type of muscular dystrophy and became less and less able to move her limbs. She sat on the bench when she arrived for therapy and waited for someone to take off her coat.

When Moti, suffering from a similar condition to Tina, became less able to do things for himself, he thought of answers. He would stand in front of the bench and shake off his coat. When it was off, he would turn round and, with a supreme effort, put the hanger over a hook. When he wanted his coat, he stood in front of the hook, put his arms in the sleeves, and then rolled his shoulders so that the coat came off the hook. He continued to do this until he needed to use a wheelchair.

The difference of determination in the two children was very marked. The difference was also seen in the playroom. Tina did not make any moves towards activities. She often asked what she should do. Though the therapist tried, over time, to get Tina to choose her own play, Tina was reluctant. She was disinclined to talk regarding her feelings about her declining strength, but accepted a wheelchair, when the time came, with, it seemed, little emotion.

Moti, on the other hand, was full of ideas when he arrived each week. He asked for the materials he needed and would involve the counsellor. He chatted about how he would need a wheelchair and about what he wanted to do while he was still mobile. When his wheelchair arrived, he accepted it willingly and described how he could use it to do things that he had not been able to do before. He spoke about the sadness he felt both for himself and his parents as his life was to be shorter than most other people's.

It is difficult to work out how motivation is achieved. In one child there can be a determination to make an effort in the most extreme circumstances and another child may refuse to think about ways in which he could do something for himself. Parents have a great deal of influence. There are those who understandably carry a burden of guilt and try to overcompensate, allowing the child to demand whatever he pleases, feeling that the child has already made sacrifices in health terms. Other parents want their child to live as normal a life as possible and treat the child as they treat other siblings, especially in behavioural issues. There are those who cannot cope with the thought of the child taking any risks and there are those who feel that the young person needs to experiment as would any other child. Being the only child can also make a difference; there is no opportunity to make comparisons of development and behaviour.

When a counsellor is working with a child who has any special need, the assessment should include parental input, as it is vital to get some idea of what they are wanting for the child. Of course, some will have unrealistic expectations, but they need to be dealt with at the outset of counselling.

Diverse learning abilities

There are some therapists who would say that therapy is not suitable for children with moderate learning difficulties. Yet some very good work has been done with such children. The process is longer than with the child of normal achievement, but there is no reason why children with learning difficulties should miss out on the opportunity to deal with some of their emotional problems. Indeed, it could be argued that for some children, their emotional needs are so weighty that they are unable to learn, not because they do not have the ability, but because there is no space in their minds for their ability to be used.

CASE EXAMPLE

Nyra
Nyra was a child who had had learning difficulties throughout her school life. She was placed in a school for children with moderate learning difficulties, but proved to be disruptive there. There was a long history of social-work involvement with the family and eventually Nyra was placed in a residential school. For the first few months, Nyra ran away on numerous occasions, but always wanted to be found and brought back to the school. She showed high anxiety all the time. Then gradually she began to trust her therapist. Little by little, she began to talk about the things that had

happened in her home and how she had been abused in a multitude of different ways. Soon Nyra was settling down into the way of life in the school. She did not learn to read well, but she was able to take part in discussions. Rather than disrupting constantly, she was able to focus occasionally. Her anxiety lessened now and again, though she still experienced agitation much of the time as a result of her neurotic vigilance. She was worried about what she was given to eat or drink; she was worried about where she was taken; fear dominated her life. It took approximately three years for Nyra to settle into a new existence; she would not trust easily, but she had trusted her therapist, who then worked with her on transferring her new-found trust to other relationships.

Nyra found learning to read laborious, but she was able to communicate satisfactorily. When her programme was changed to help her recognize labels on food and to sort out money for purchases, she managed to acquire enough literacy and numeracy to live in a school flat.

When Nyra left the residential school, she went to college and was able to get employment. She needed some support in maintaining a satisfactory life, but she gained enough life skills for more than survival. She was one of the children who would never be able to be rid of her past, but she could improve her lot in life for the future.

The therapist needs to provide materials that may be suitable for younger children. Where these are available, often older children regress to playing with toys which they missed in their earlier years. One of the good things about keeping all the things that belong in the playroom from being taken elsewhere is that it allows the child to regress within the therapeutic space, without compromising their interactions outside the therapy. The child client realizes that the playroom is a special space in which special work can be done, but he can return to his place in the external world. This is important where counselling takes place in schools. The playroom needs to be containing while the child is there, but also kept apart from the child's other learning space.

Nyra's learning difficulties were triggered by her anxiety, as there was such a degree of this that it took all her energy to contain. Children's emotional needs present in different ways.

CASE EXAMPLE

Eileen

Eileen had been snatched from her pram when she was a baby and taken to her father's home, whereupon her mother had tried unsuccessfully to get her daughter back. The couple had split up before Eileen was born. Eileen had then been through a succession of foster placements and her early life was traumatized by various incidents. When Eileen was 14, she was offered therapy under the supervision of a psychiatrist.

Eileen played with dolls and showed her caring warmth in cradling them and using feeding bottles. At times, she would drink from the bottles herself. She talked about mothering herself and taking care of her own needs. Symbolically, her play was helping her to feed herself in a way that helped her to feel that her needs could be satisfied.

If Eileen's friends had known about her play, she would have been unable to face them. They would not have understood the need for her regression, yet it was an important factor for Eileen. The confidentiality of the playroom is essential. There can be no confusion in this important element.

Diverse cultures

Where there are major differences in culture, older children and adolescents need to explore with the therapist how they feel about the difference. Younger children tend to be more accepting of difference, as they have not yet met as much prejudice. However, if they mention difference, the therapist needs to hear what the child is saying. The therapist is not in a very different place. Both she and the client are learning together how to relate to each other and how to deal with issues that arise. There is a temptation to see children with a difference in culture as belonging to a group. But that must be dismissed and the child or young person not expected to carry the collective assumption, whatever that might be. The client might also have assumptions about therapists, and the individual does not have to carry those!

There is always the age difference when working with children and the therapist does have a power that should not be present in adult counselling. The child's safety is paramount and the therapist cannot relinquish her adult authority over any matter that would endanger the child. This makes it more difficult in some ways. The therapist has to be more careful not to abuse that power.

There are inequalities in so many aspects of life. We are shaped by our culture and language. We need to explore who we are in the light of our differences, but never feel that our way of being is the norm. Whiteness is something that is not often explored as one of many colours, but there is a need to shake ourselves out of the assumptions that are archaic and institutionalized. The therapist needs to welcome and appreciate each child's attitudes and not accept them with resignation. Each therapy is a sharing of a new journey with a new travelling companion, who has come from a different place and is going somewhere different. We have the privilege of sharing a little part of that journey. All our meetings need to have a fluidity that allows thoughts to run freely between the two.

Good supervision is a prerequisite for all counselling, but when the therapist's clients include children with special needs, the support needed is greater. The work is emotionally draining and sometimes a supervisory session might be required immediately after a difficult session. If there is no possibility of this, the therapist might feel that she cannot take on some extreme work. The child is then denied therapy and another difference is created. There are also implications for other people in the therapy centre – other therapists, receptionists and anyone who may come into contact with the special child. Children who are volatile and likely to show hostility, violence and self-harm can be frightening, and training is required on how to handle situations that might occur on the way to or from the therapy room. With special needs, there is more at stake. There is something in human nature that withdraws from those who are different and counsellors often feel that somehow they will do more harm to someone who is already disabled. If this thinking is pursued and such children are refused therapy, these children are being done a dis-service. Their difference is then compounded by another difference. They are denied the right to a method of treatment, to which their more fortunate peers have access.

Counsellors need to take into account every aspect of counselling children. Because many other professionals working with children have clear ideas as to the developmental milestones that a child will pass, they have a tendency to see children as 'normal' or as 'causes for concern'. The therapist must not fall into the trap of assuming that a child referred will be at any particular stage on the spectrum of developmental tasks or emotional growth. Having one's own children, of about the same age as clients, could be detrimental to the counsellor having a clear space for the child client. Comparisons with any other child should be avoided at all costs. Children who require therapy are often those whose configuration of maturing has no real pattern, but there are small cultivated patches with other areas uncharted. To allow the child to come into the counselling room with his own internal world, and his own way of expressing it, is essential for work to take place.

Counsellor–client matching

Working with young people can be fraught with difficulty. There are so many vulnerable youngsters, and these are the children and adolescents who are likely to need therapy. The counsellor needs to know her own position, but not to let this encroach on the young person. There are some schools of thought that would like to give every youngster a counsellor closely matched to the client's background culture, gender, faith, sexual orientation and race. There may be times when the client is unable to trust someone of a particular grouping and one aspect may be easy to deal with, but there are also assumptions made that are false. If we were to try to match counsellors and clients, there might be assumptions on both sides that there was sameness that actually might not exist. Not every woman counsellor will be persuaded by feminist values; there will be some male therapists who are more feminist than their female counterparts. Not all ethnic clients will feel marginalized, though some will. Each client has to be considered as an individual in every aspect of his life. The counsellor's task is to find out the client's way of conceptualizing his experiences and to work within that frame of reference, not her own. Adolescents might request some sameness in a counsellor with the expectation that they could take the power in the therapy. This omnipotence could make the beginning of therapy more difficult. Younger children generally do not request any matching, and older children's prejudice (or that of their parents) could be fed if their requests were fulfilled.

The main basis for the counsellor–client relationship is the trust that is built up between them. The client explores the counsellor as the counsellor explores the young person. Young children can be fascinated by the counsellor's features and will often say openly what adults would not dare to voice. In many ways, this makes it easier to talk with the child about the difference.

CASE EXAMPLE

Katrina

Katrina was 3 years old, and when she met her therapist she kept pointing at his nose. She held her own nose and at times she pushed her fingers into her nostrils. When she picked up the black and white dolls she exclaimed about the black doll: 'No nose.' The therapist was able to talk to Katrina about the fact that she was interested in noses and how their noses differed. Katrina wanted 'a flat nose with big holes', because hers was 'sticking out with no holes'. The therapist watched as Katrina put large play-doh noses on heads that she made. Then she flattened them, saying 'Nice nose.'

Later in the therapy, it emerged that Katrina had been alarmed by the pictures of Pinocchio, whose nose had grown when he told lies. Her father had pulled her nose in fun, but she had taken it to mean that she had done something bad.

When she saw the therapist's African nose, she thought her therapist must be good and her own nose shape was because she was bad. The therapist worked with pictures of children with different shaped noses; Katrina was fascinated with the pictures and through this was enabled to separate nose shape from naughtiness.

When children notice difference, it is an ideal way of finding out their perceptions. Sadly, some very young children come to therapy with prejudices that they do not understand, but which have been handed on to them by adults. This can be distressing for the therapist; it might be an opportunity to put into the playroom materials that can bring out further discussion.

The counsellor does not have to develop expertise in any one formula or theory that would dictate how the work is done, but be receptive to all the workings of the client. Counsellors often worry that they will be out of their depth; that is because they are thinking of themselves as the experts and as the client coming to them for wisdom. This is not counselling! Counselling enables the client to tell his story and to do the explaining.

When counselling children and young people, there is an added difficulty in that counsellors are tempted to assume that their clients are not able to make interpretations. This can lead to the counsellor feeling in a position of knowledge and power; however, it is likely that there will be a great deal of the time spent in 'not knowing'.

There might be a tendency to suppose that if a counsellor has some identification with the child client there would be a more ready rapport between them. But this is not necessarily so. More of a danger would be to suppose that the experience of the counsellor would be similar in some way, when in fact the situation of the child could be vastly different. To try to make an 'external' fit for the client is not important. What is important is that the counsellor and client establish a real relationship as well as the transference relationship. Sameness and difference are both essential for human life. As a child grows, so he needs repetition, but also the differences that allow progression. The child who can only repeat cannot expand in any way. The child who can tolerate difference can use the variations to explore new ways of being.

Summary

1. There are differences between any two people, as we are all unique.
2. Diversity needs to be acknowledged, but in counselling it can be used to enrich both the counsellor and the client. Children teach us a great deal.

3. Special children face various difficulties. Emotional needs are the main focus, but the therapist needs to take into account pertinent physical and learning factors, so that children are not further disadvantaged.
4. We have highlighted the need for the therapist to hear from the child and not make assumptions.
5. All counselling work has to be undertaken within a framework of ethical practice, as the next chapter will show.

7

ETHICAL ISSUES

Overview

The Children Act (1989) gives children rights and allows parents to have a say in the treatment their children undergo. Whenever conflicts arise, it is generally accepted that whatever is done must be 'in the child's best interests'. The dilemma is to know how to identify these 'best interests' of the child: giving the child a choice, for instance, might seem the best thing for the child, but if the choice is a real one, he may choose something that is not in his best interests. However, to take away his choice would disempower him, with unknown consequences for his self-esteem and ability to cope in the long term. These thorny issues are addressed in this chapter, but often raise more questions than they answer.

Any person having direct contact with children needs to have an enhanced disclosure check carried out by the authorities. Child protection is an emotive subject, but it is important that counsellors, who will work one-to-one with children, recognize the need for police checks. Every agency that works with children will have a scheme in place. Most counselling centres now conform to this practice, as vulnerable adults also need protection.

Children and the law

Children have rights; in recent years there have been a number of attempts to clarify the law with regard to child and parental rights. With regard to counselling, children have a right to make a confidential relationship with a counsellor, without parental consent, providing the child has an understanding of what counselling is and can use it to his benefit.

The Children Act was established to give children rights. The difficulty is that the Act can be contested at various points. No system will ever cover all needs, but there were key principles by which anyone working with children was advised to act. These were:

- the welfare of the child must be the paramount concern;
- the child has a right to a family experience in which both parents have responsibility for his upbringing;
- parents who have children with special needs should be encouraged and supported in being responsible for their children;
- intervention should be made when a child is in danger;
- courts should ensure that there are no delays when children are involved;
- children should be informed about decisions about them taken by others;
- parents have rights and authority and duty to care for the child and to use those rights and authority for the best interests of the child, allowing him to live a physically and emotionally healthy life;
- parents have responsibilities even if their children no longer live with them; they should receive information and be part of the decision-making.[43]

Within the entangled world of relationships that constitute some families, it is sometimes difficult to know what is in the best interests of the child.

CASE EXAMPLE

Sam

Sam was 6 years old when she disclosed to a therapist that the foster home in which she was living was causing great distress. There had been several older boys who had come into the family for short stays. Two boys, in particular, had harassed her. They had tied her down on her bed and proceeded to sexually abuse her.

The matter was reported to the police and social services; the child came under the care of the court, which made a ruling that the child should no longer have contact with the therapist to whom the allegations had been confided. The reason given was that Sam might be influenced to go over the story, thus making her more sure of the details of what took place. The thinking was that this would give her an unfair advantage over the boys.

This meant that though Sam was now being subjected to investigations, which were causing her anguish, she was not given access to the security of the therapist's time and place. Sam felt that she was being punished for talking about the incidents and withdrew into herself. She was provided with a different foster placement, which she also interpreted as another sign that she should not have spoken out.

By the time the court was able to deal with the allegations, Sam was hardly coping; she could not be persuaded to speak and her school reports showed that she had changed from being a lively little girl into an isolated and sad child. The boys, in this incident, admitted that they had abused Sam and though *they* were then put into a treatment programme, it was a long time before Sam was able to have any therapy.

When Sam needed her therapy most it was denied. It had to be stopped immediately, which made her feel that even her therapist had let her down. Although the therapist made representations to the Social Services department, there was no relenting, even to allow Sam to have an ending session.

The difficulty in this case was that the needs of three children were at stake. All three needed consideration and it would seem that the boys' needs for treatment were immediately recognized, whereas Sam's need may have been interpreted as the cessation of the abuse. Danger from abuse was no longer present, so in that sense her need was met.

Sometimes there is a difference in the views held around gender. The perpetration of abuse is alarming, particularly in boy adolescents, whom it is feared will go on to abuse as adults. Victims draw out different emotions to do with hurt and sorrow. These feelings do not necessarily act as a spur to such swift action as fear.

It would be helpful if every child, either abuser or abused, was able to have a supportive person to think through with the child (and, if appropriate, a caring adult) what has happened, the reasons for the abuse and what the child wants to happen.

There are times when children are not permitted to have therapy; for instance, when a court case is pending, particularly when there has been an allegation of sexual abuse. This is at a time when the child really needs to be able to talk to somebody in confidence. There is suspicion around counsellors; a fear that somehow the counsellor will influence the child and the child's story will be contaminated. A properly trained therapist would not be influencing a child, but allowing the child the space to talk about his fears and anxieties. Children who have been traumatized find it very difficult to talk about the events. When they do, it is usually distressing.

CASE EXAMPLE

Freda

Freda was a shy 10-year-old. Sometimes she would shake so much with anger that she turned in on herself. She found it difficult to speak about anything in her past. The school she was attending asked for her to be given a special placement and Freda was terrified when she arrived at the new school. After a year, Freda confided in the school counsellor that she had been part of a group of people who had sexually abused her from a young age. This had taken place in the context of a group of adults, whose naked abuse of each other she was also forced to observe.

The child's story was told over a number of weeks, with many tears and silences. When a child is able to get to this point, it is important that it is handled very sensitively. There was a whole mass of evidence and the person working with the child thought that one episode in the story was probably too bizarre to be true. However, in discussions with the police, they verified the facts of the story. The school counsellor was called as an expert witness for the court case which followed. During the preparation of the case, the solicitor told the school that he had to change the typist every ten minutes when the notes were being typed, because the child's story distressed the secretaries so much.

The magistrates said that they had never handled such difficult material and listened to one parent's own experience of earlier abuse. They decided that in such circumstances, the parent could not be expected to protect her child. The court also ruled that the child had learning difficulties and so could not give reliable evidence. It was one of the parents who had told the court that his daughter could not be believed as she had learning difficulties. The child on one occasion said she had been given fish and chips and at a consequent interview had said that she had been given a burger and chips on the way back from an abusive event. This was cited as evidence that the child's witness was unreliable. This child, who had risked so much to tell her story, was badly let down. The parent was permitted to go on allowing the child to be the victim of horrendous abuse by many different people. The welfare of the child was certainly not paramount. After some time, the child ran away from home and was eventually taken into care, but not before an increasing number of abusive occurrences.

Freda's parents were victims of childhood abuse and no doubt had huge needs, but Freda's current needs were not addressed by the court. The difficulty for the court was that it was presented with very explicit material about the previous generation. This needed addressing, yet the case was about Freda's safety.

The perceived unreliability of children's witness statements, particularly for those who have learning difficulties, is a real matter for concern. The Children's Panel, in Scotland, the equivalent of court proceedings in England and Wales, gives greater opportunity for the child to be represented by a supportive adult and for there to be several people in discussion about the best interests of the child. Also, in this system, the child is taken to a friendlier environment for decisions to be offered to those involved.

Referrers

The Children Act allows parents to have a say in the treatment their children undergo. This means that there will be children who may not gain access to the treatment they need. Some parents do not have the necessary time to set aside for one child, particularly if there are a number of siblings. If the parent is the one who brings the child for therapy, there may be completely unrealistic expectations, whereas others will be asking for whatever help is available, with hope rather than impatience. Some parents want their children to 'be cured in six weeks'. What they mean by 'cure' is that the child will learn how to conform quickly and behave in a way that the parent desires.

Therapists need to explore the parents' wishes and understanding of the therapeutic process. There is no 'cure'; parents need to know that if the child has painful issues to address he may well go through a period when things will become more difficult. Helping a parent to realize that a child's behaviour is not just to be bloody-minded, but that behaviour comes from within the child, as an expression of what is inside, is part of the introductory process. If behaviour is distressing to those around him, then the child is likely to be experiencing internal distress.

The therapist's task is to find a way for the child to access the distress in a safe environment; to help him to understand the causes of the distress and how to cope with the feelings aroused in an appropriate way that is not destructive to himself.

Working with children requires that the parents or the referrer be taken into the equation. Although the child is the client, the young child cannot bring himself to therapy up to a certain age. This is another difference in working with children. The adult who chooses therapy is able to make his own decisions; to stay away from therapy or to end. But the child is not in a position to do much of the choosing.

He cannot get himself to therapy unless brought by an adult. Unless the counsellor manages to get the full co-operation of the adult, the child's therapy will suffer.

Therapists also need to remember that the child is always part of other systems, the most important being where the child is placed. It is vital to obtain background information about the place where the child spends most of his time and the relational qualities between the child and the carers. The other people must never be treated as the client, but the client is always within a context. This is discussed further in Chapter 9. Adults are able to communicate to the counsellor the different nuances in relationships, but a child cannot do this to the same degree. The counsellor needs to work with other agencies also involved with the child and to understand the roles of the different helpers in order to work as part of the child's whole world.

Confidentiality

The question of confidentiality is particularly complex when working with children and young people. Some agencies have specific guidelines as to when confidentiality may be broken. Such incidents might be sexual abuse, physical abuse, threat of suicide or self-harm. Where the agency has clear guidance, the counsellor must abide by this in every circumstance. Her contract with the agency forms an agreement to abide by these conditions. Where the agency allows for individual therapists to use their own judgement, there is greater need for the therapist to work out the strategies she will employ in the course of her work. Every client, whether child or young person, needs to know from the beginning of the therapy what steps will be taken in certain situations. It is quite shocking for the client to trust the counsellor and to believe that the therapist will accept anything within the confines of the counselling room and then to suddenly discover that the counsellor is talking about the need to break confidentiality at the painful point of disclosure. Where it is written into a contract or has been noted at the start of the counselling, a reminder can clarify the situation at the time of the admission. This makes it very clear for older clients.

With young children, where play therapy is being used, it is still necessary to put into simple terms to the child that if the therapist believes anything is happening that is not keeping the child safe, she will need to speak to someone else about finding a way to protect the child. The counsellor will need to know the agency to which information can be passed to secure the safety of a child who might be at risk. Each agency will have a child protection policy which will include this. Usually a named person will contact the relevant authorities.

All of this will be of no use, unless the child can understand what is said. For each child, the therapist has to consider the level of understanding, the language used by the child, the pattern of the context in which the child lives and the names of those who are important in the child's life.

CASE EXAMPLE

Alison

When Alison told her counsellor about abuse by her grandfather, the counsellor reported it to the agency's child protection co-ordinator. The co-ordinator knew that the child's grandfather was not living near the family home and that mother was a caring and capable parent. Letting the child go home was not an issue. The child needed more time with the counsellor before the matter could be easily revealed to the mother. Social Services, knowing the counselling centre and the co-ordinator's work, asked what the counselling centre would like to do about the child. The co-ordinator asked for more time for the counsellor to work with the child; for the child's mother to be invited to attend a meeting with the child and counsellor when the child felt prepared and for the mother to be offered her own counselling to deal with this problem. Social Services accepted this plan and suggested that the mother could be offered an appointment with the department if she required further help.

The counsellor continued to work with the child and in a later session met with the child and the mother. The child was enabled to tell her story to her mother, who understandably was very upset. She accepted the offer of counselling for herself and made sure that the child was not taken to her grandfather's house. Mother was enabled to speak with her father and to arrange visits to her mother when father absented himself.

In this situation there was much more work to be done, but it could be carried out without the threat of court hearings or punishment. Neither the child nor her grandmother was made to feel that they were being punished for the grandfather's misdeeds. This freed the child to talk more openly about the abusive relationship, her sense of betrayal by her grandfather and of her feelings about needing to see her grandmother because she wanted to keep close ties with her, but now knowing that she would never have to be on her own with her grandfather again. Social Services were able to meet with the mother and discuss the abuse when the mother was receiving support, which enabled her to talk more freely about her father and how the issue could be addressed without making the child feel that she had caused a problem.

In recent years, there seems to be a much more balanced approach towards children who have been abused. When the incidence of sexual abuse was first talked about, there were reactions in caring agencies that were not helpful to the child. First and foremost, the child who has been abused needs to feel supported. It is often just as traumatic for the child to remember the abuse as it was when the act was committed. It is essential for the therapist to believe in the child's essential truthfulness. There may be inaccuracies in the story, but the child is telling it in the way that makes sense to him. Even if part of the story has been fabricated, there is a reason for the fabrication.

CASE EXAMPLE

Ned

Ned was 14 years old and presenting most of the teachers at his secondary school with problems. When they tried to discipline him, he would sit on a desk at the front of the classroom and hurl abuse at the teacher. Because of this, it was necessary to have him removed from the classroom on a number of occasions each week. The parents were asked to discuss Ned with the form teacher. Ned's father agreed to the meeting, but his mother said that father could sort out Ned's problems. The school then suspended Ned and he was referred for psychiatric assessment. But there was a two-year wait for an appointment at the clinic, so Ned's parents asked a counsellor to arrange appointments for him. Ned willingly went to the appointments and told the counsellor about many sexual encounters in which he had engaged with girls at school and at his youth club. These stories came out one after the other and there were discrepancies in the things Ned said. When the counsellor pointed out the discrepancies, Ned covered himself with more and more outrageous tales. The counsellor began to feel uneasy about his work with Ned. He tried to confront Ned in a kindly way, suggesting that sometimes young people have a real need to voice their anxieties, but sometimes the anxiety is expressed by overemphasis on some aspects of the story. With this gentle suggestion, Ned began to sob uncontrollably. He admitted that the story of his being raped by a gang of youths at the youth club had been fictitious. The counsellor continued to reassure Ned that there was a reason behind his need to tell this tale and that, given time, Ned might be able to discover what lay behind it himself.

Ned wanted to be a journalist and his counsellor suggested he might like to write something between sessions. On the next occasion, Ned produced a scrappy piece of paper, on which he had written a story about a monkey who was kept in a cage and only allowed out of the cage to do tricks for a harsh master. When he was in the cage, the monkey felt lonely and cowered in his bed, wondering when he would be turned out again and made to do his circus tricks. If he grumbled he would be beaten, so he always conformed.

After a great deal of work with Ned, over two years, the real dilemma became clear to Ned and he was able to tell the counsellor about how his father left the house for a night shift each evening. Ned was then asked to sleep with his mother, as she was lonely. His mother made threats to him if he did not satisfy her sexually when she wanted her pleasure. This meant that Ned, too, was able to hold his mother to ransom, so that it became the pattern that she gave in to his wishes, as he could threaten to tell his father what was going on.

Ned was 16 before his appointment with the psychiatric department was offered. The family was asked to attend, but again only father was willing to go along with Ned. The clinic explained that Ned was now of an age when the clinic would be passing on his case to the adult department. He attended a few sessions, but they were few and far between. Ned left home and married a young girl whom he despised. It was his desperate attempt to get away from his mother. He went to live many miles from the family home. Ned had difficulty having any intimacy with his wife, but the unsatisfactory partnership continued.

This enmeshed situation was too difficult for Ned to talk about for a long time. He was acting out in the classroom his power over other authority figures. His mother had put him in the position of being able to manipulate her for his own ends and she complied for fear of being betrayed. When Ned's teachers did not conform, he became abusive as he did not know how to respond to adults not doing his bidding.

Social Services were alerted to Ned's difficulties, but Ned would never incriminate his mother, which was understandable. He always pleaded that she was good to him and cited all the things that she did for him, without mentioning his blackmail in the situation.

It is important that the child realizes that the therapist will provide confidentiality, so that he can discuss sensitive information and talk about things that are difficult. In some agencies, the child is rightly told at the beginning of counselling that the counsellor will report anything about sexual abuse. This may well warn the child that the things that are troubling him most cannot be brought into the counselling room without disclosure being made to other agencies. In other situations, agency rules require that a counsellor warn a client when approaching sexual issues, that if the client proceeds with the story, then referral will be made. This might well prevent the child from further informing the counsellor. There has to be value in the child being able to disclose. A sensitive counsellor will then negotiate the next stage with the child. Rather than putting the child off, it is much more helpful to engage with the child in thinking about the path that should be followed. The child can be informed by the counsellor that the situation is unsafe and that she would want it to be made safe, enquiring with the young person how safety could be achieved. Where there is no immediate danger to the child, or where the sexual abuse was in the past and no longer being perpetuated, there is no reason why there should be a knee-jerk reaction. The child will benefit much more from a calm, reasoned interchange with the counsellor. Even young children can understand the concept of being safe and in many cases will be quite happy for another person to receive the given information. It depends on the age of the child, his ability to communicate, and the agency requirements as to whether the counsellor has a role to play in this sharing of information. But at all times, the child client has a right to know what is happening. There should be no communication with other agencies without telling the child. This would lead to a breakdown of trust between the counsellor and the client, which would hinder any further work.

The counsellor must take responsibility for the decisions she is making. Where the employing agency has policies that she is following, it is wise for the counsellor to tell the child that she is taking the decision. To suggest that the agency demands her response is to suggest to the child that she would not necessarily take such an action if she had the choice. This might allow the child to think that the counsellor would collude in taking no action and would change the relationship that has been achieved. The counsellor wants to have this in the room and not put outside to an external locus. Any reaction that the child shows needs to be addressed within the relationship. Counsellors can be wary of taking their responsibility for fear of spoiling the relationship, but the opposite is true. If the child has placed trust in the counsellor, the trust is betrayed and the child uncontained if the counsellor withdraws and cites the agency as being responsible.

CASE EXAMPLE

Tyrone

Tyrone was 12 years old when his mother asked for counselling. He was offered sessions on certain conditions. His stepfather was serving a prison sentence for the sexual abuse of Tyrone; his mother was upset that the abuse had occurred, but was annoyed that Tyrone's disclosure to teachers at school and then to the social worker had meant the sentencing of her husband. There had been no contact since he had been imprisoned. It was agreed with the social worker and Tyrone that any further sexual abuse would be discussed with the social worker. The counsellor made sure that Tyrone understood that the normal boundaries of confidentiality were not being offered to him, because of the arrangements with Social Services. But the counsellor explained to Tyrone that they needed to have a clear picture of what would happen. So he suggested that every time there was any communication between him and the social worker, Tyrone would be told exactly what passed between them. This was to be done by written information from the counsellor to the social worker, being discussed with Tyrone and his agreement secured that it could be shared. This arrangement worked well until on one occasion, after the stepfather had been released, the social worker was convinced that Tyrone was seeing him, against the court ruling. The social worker informed Tyrone that the counsellor had informed her that Tyrone had admitted this had been happening. Needless to say, the counsellor was extremely angry that the social worker had not only lied, but completely destroyed the trust that had taken a long time to build between himself and Tyrone. He complained to the social worker, who said she needed to get at the truth. A complaint was also made to the senior social worker.

This case shows how agencies can renege on their obligations when working with a child who is receiving counselling. The counsellor had tried to set up a transparent way of allowing the client a space to talk, while also protecting the client's trust. The relationship was never the same again and it was not long before Tyrone missed appointments and then ended the therapy. At the point where the breakdown occurred, Tyrone had not said he had seen his stepfather, but he was beginning to talk of being tired of trying to manage his own feelings alongside his mother's feelings for his stepfather. He was weary of the conflict of trying to know whether to go with his own wishes not to have the man in the house again and upset his mother, or whether to let his mother's wishes be uppermost and try to live in a detached way in the same house. With these conflicting feelings and the onset of puberty, this adolescent needed to address his identity as a separate person. He had trusted the counsellor enough to uncover some of the deep conflicts of the past abuse – his sense of pleasure as well as his anger – but the tenuous relationship was spoiled by another 'mother'-figure deciding that her needs were more important than his needs. This was adding to his feeling of being thwarted by adults.

Parents often have difficulties with confidentiality, even though the parameters of the counselling are spelt out to them before the counselling begins. Some will question their children as to what they have said in their sessions, though the counsellor has told them that to do this is unhelpful. The child is at liberty to tell any other person what happens in a session; it is not to be a secret between counsellor and child. But he should be allowed privacy if he chooses. It is the therapist, who has given assurance to the child that the counselling room is a safe place where the child can speak of anything; she will not be repeating the information to parents, teachers or other people. It is not necessary with young children to explain the situation of confidentiality in supervision, but it is important to explain this to older children.

Parents can be particularly sensitive to the fact that their child is talking to somebody else, particularly if their own relationship with the child has been strained and communication has broken down. The counsellor must never use the trust built between herself and the child to become competitive with the parent. The counsellor is a professional working for the good of the child and the best outcome will be for the child to be able to better communicate with family members. If a good relationship is established in the counselling room, then there is great investment in keeping alive the hope that such a relationship can then be built or rebuilt with the persons where there have been rifts in communication.

CASE EXAMPLE

Xanthe

Xanthe was seen as a problem in her family. She was attending a college, but was not willing to study. She stayed out late, used alcohol to excess and consistently taunted her older sister who had recently moved out of the family home, to a flat that was being made into a home for herself and her partner. Xanthe had always been a bit of a tomboy.

From the outset of the counselling, Xanthe arrived in a duffle coat, with a long, knitted woollen scarf and a trilby hat that she wore down over her eyes. The counsellor immediately liked Xanthe. Xanthe was her own person and found no trouble at all in putting her feelings into words. She had not wanted to go to college, but her parents had insisted that it would be in her best interests. Her sister had done well at school and had gone through university as a good student. She now had a good job and was settled in every way. Xanthe presented as being very restless, wanting to achieve something for herself, not wanting to replicate her sister's success. She needed something of her own that was different. She wanted to work evenings and weekends as a waitress, but her parents thought that would be detrimental to her studies. They spent their time trying to persuade Xanthe to study and she spent her time at home arguing with her parents that they did not listen to her.

When Xanthe was asked how she could move forward in her life, she admitted that nothing could be done unless she could talk to her parents. Afraid that she could not do this because of the set patterns of behaviour in the family, she asked if the counsellor would have a session with the whole family. The counsellor had training in family therapy and agreed to Xanthe's request.

In the first two sessions, Xanthe showed some very infantile behaviour, whining when she spoke. Her father dismissed her whining and said he could only listen if she would say something different, as he had heard all her complaints before. Mother was at a loss as to how to intervene to break the stalemate. The older sister said very little, but was obviously the apple of her father's eye. During the second session, Xanthe challenged her father that he had really wanted a son and that to have had one daughter was acceptable to him, but when she was born, he had been disappointed. Her father sat very still and did not reply. Mother began to make excuses for her husband, saying that it had been difficult for her husband, who had lost his mother just before Xanthe was born. He had found this loss impossible to cope with, and had had very little to do with the new baby.

Xanthe became angry at this and told her father that he had been a father to her sister but not to her. The counsellor suggested that Xanthe's father should have his own counselling to address the bereavement issues which were still troubling him, but wondered what he felt about Xanthe's anger. He remained passive.

In the third family session, Xanthe was quiet and the mother tried to make conversation and jump into the silences on a few occasions. The counsellor pointed out that Xanthe's mother seemed to resist silence and perhaps she was worried as to what might occur if the silence continued. She then left a space. After a few minutes, Xanthe knocked off her trilby, stood up, went over to her father and hugged him. She told him she loved him and that all she had ever wanted from him was that he loved her as he loved her sister. Father was completely taken by surprise and broke down. He shed tears for quite some time and said how much he wished he could change things, but he had been caught up in trying to replicate the good experience he had had with his older daughter and he had not allowed her to be herself. He was frightened of the unknown with her. Xanthe reminded him of his mother, who had died just before Xanthe was born, but he could not cope with the feelings of grief that still overwhelmed him when he thought of his deceased parent.

Xanthe and her parents then talked about Xanthe's future in different terms. She had a plan to work in a restaurant and to learn the catering trade. She loved cooking and her parents said how good she was at preparing delicious meals for them at home. They relented and suggested that she could do the college catering course instead of the secretarial one on which she had enrolled.

Xanthe did very well in the catering trade. Two years later she was putting to the bank manager a business plan for opening a restaurant in partnership with an experienced chef.

In the above example, Xanthe was ready to try out new ways of relating to her father. The family had labelled her as the family problem; Xanthe was allowing herself to *be* the family problem. When she was empowered to speak up, as a member of the family and not its problem, she became aware that she was part of a family system and that the system needed to change to function adequately. She was the catalyst in helping the family to reassess what was happening. It was Xanthe who helped the family to change its way of being. She needed the counsellor to affirm her position in the family as a young person with ambition and not just a problem to everybody.

In court

Therapeutic confidentiality is recognized by the courts, but it is not protected by the law. This means that a court is likely to be sympathetic to the counsellor and client relationship, but there is no legal status of this position. If a judge subpoenas a counsellor to give a report, then this has to be produced. If the counsellor is called to give evidence, she must appear. However, a solicitor interested in a case cannot demand reports or court appearances; nor can the police.

CASE EXAMPLE

Robert

Robert was 7 when his mother asked a counsellor to offer him therapy sessions. She had been left with Robert by the child's father. She was aware that Robert now only had her input and she was concerned that Robert might get a jaundiced view of his father from her. She wanted to avoid this and she felt that Robert needed to be able to tell somebody outside the family what he felt about her. He had used his father in this way before his father left. Mother had indicated that father knew Robert was attending therapy and that father had been quite angry that arrangements had been made without his prior consent.

After a few weeks, Robert's father came to the counselling centre and demanded to talk to the counsellor. He was a police officer and he tried to use this status to say that he had a right to know what his son was disclosing in the counselling sessions. The counsellor knew that she did not have to disclose anything to the police officer, but as a father he was entitled to as much information as the mother, because he had shared legal guardianship of the child at that time.

The counsellor explained what therapy was about and the confidentiality of the child's material. Robert's father kept insisting that the law was on his side and that the counsellor could not listen to what the child was saying without him being party to the information. Eventually, he was calmed by the counsellor stating that if there were anything that needed to be passed on to any party, both he and the mother would receive exactly the same information.

As a safeguard, the counsellor spoke to the agency's legal adviser, to report the incident and explain what had been said. The solicitor agreed that the counsellor had handled the situation appropriately and that the father had no legal right to other information unless he took the matter to court and the court ruled that he could have access to further notes.

Counsellors keep clinical notes on their clients. These act as an aide-mémoire for the work and are kept securely by the counsellor or the agency. It is important that counsellors realize that these notes could be requested by a court. It is not acceptable for the counsellor to write one set of scanty notes for the agency and then to keep other notes. All notes that are written could become evidence. Although the likelihood of this happening is small, counsellors should bear this in mind when they commit anything to paper. There are regulations for keeping any records on computers, and counsellors who wish to use this format for client records need to register with the Data Protection Information Commissioner's Office.

There may be occasions when the therapist is unhappy holding information about a client. This should be discussed with a supervisor or agency manager before any breach of confidentiality is made. Some agencies have a policy that suicidal clients are told that the counsellor will inform a medical practitioner if they are concerned that the client might take his own life. Other agencies leave this to the individual counsellor's discretion. With children, there is much more responsibility placed upon the counsellor. Young children have the right to be protected and sometimes need an adult to intervene when the child is not safe. This would apply to young people threatening to harm themselves. The important thing is that the young person needs to know that the counsellor is going to proceed in a certain way. With an adolescent, it is always better to try to persuade the young person to contact a health professional himself. This may involve the counsellor allowing use of the telephone to make an appointment. With a younger child it would be informing the person collecting the child of the distress that the child was experiencing and asking the escort to ensure that the child received the necessary help.

Professional negligence

In these days of prolific litigation, counsellors working with children need to understand the principle of professional negligence. This term refers to the fact that a counsellor would be deemed to have attained a reasonable level of competence to work with clients. Where a child might be harmed after receiving therapy, a court suing the counsellor would have to prove that the harm was due to the lack of care by the counsellor and not by any other contributing circumstances. If the counsellor were to offer advice which was acted upon by the client, who was harmed by taking the advice, there would be a clear-cut case of causation. But counsellors from psychoanalytic backgrounds do not offer advice. However, counsellors can testify to the fact that clients often return commenting that they have 'taken the counsellor's advice' and made some kind of change in their lives. The perception of the client is that the idea came from the counselling session and therefore was from the counsellor. Children also have a sense of reality from their own perception and their reality may not be the hard facts, but the counsellor is always working with the child's perception, as it is this experience that creates the feelings. Therapists do not work with cold facts, but the feelings.

It can be devastating to be the subject of an investigation, whether it is legal or professional. The counsellor needs to be able to answer in herself the questions of what she is doing and why she is using the strategy she has chosen. If she has the assurance that she can answer these questions, in the unlikely event of a client's therapy being called into question, she is likely to have a reasonable case. Professional bodies offer legal advice; in the early stages of any proceedings, the counsellor should contact the legal department of the professional body to seek advice. Some agencies have their own legal advisers who would offer the same service.

Maintaining boundaries in counsellor–client relationships

There needs to be an understanding about the place of therapeutic intervention. The therapist seeing a child will not engage with the child outside the counselling room. Because of the dependence of the child on others, collaboration with other members of the child's family should not be made in any other capacity. There is a role in pastoral care for there to be more contact, but in counselling, the boundaries have to be clearly defined. Counsellors are sometimes approached by friends and acquaintances to engage with families known to them. Any referral needs to go through the normal chan-nels. There has to be professionalism throughout the process. This can be difficult when a teacher trains as a counsellor and wants to use her skills in the school.

CASE EXAMPLE

Paula

Paula, a teacher, who had trained as a children's counsellor, had been given one day a week by her head teacher to see children for therapy; the clients were selected by the head teacher and special needs co-ordinator and were those who were difficult to contain in class situations. After consultation with a supervisor, the teacher put in the proviso that she could not give therapy sessions to children who attended her academic classes, as the boundaries between her being a teacher and a counsellor would confuse the children. The counselling with one particular child was progressing, until the day the teacher had to supervise a detention group. She found that the child she was seeing for therapy presented himself in the group. There was nothing she could do at this point, but the therapeutic relationship was destroyed. The child hurled abuse at the teacher for letting him down. There was no restoration possible for this child and the work could not continue.

The above example underlines the boundaries that need to be kept in order for work to proceed. It could be argued that a child needs to go through the disillusionment phase, having built up trust with an adult. But that has to be contained within the same relationship, or it does not make any sense to the child. Just as the idealized parent has to let the child become aware of her failings in a gradual manner, so the therapist has to allow frustration at the appropriate times. To be presented with the parent or therapist in a totally different context is to break up the pattern that the child is building.

Children are naturally curious and they will ask questions. Young teenagers will sometimes quiz the therapist to try to find out about her personal life. There are some questions that can be answered in a way that does not disclose personal information but can satisfy the enquiry. A young child may notice a therapist's wedding ring and comment. 'That says that I am married' might be the response. But to talk about being married would not be appropriate. The child might go on to talk about the significance of a ring or of another relationship. The space needs to be taken up with the child's reason for raising the issue and not the therapist's material.

CASE EXAMPLE

Colleen

Colleen was 16 and she was very inquisitive about the counsellor's internal life. This was exemplified when Colleen demanded to know whether the counsellor had undergone a hysterectomy. It would have been totally inappropriate for the client to have this information. What was more important was that the client's thoughts around the internal aspects of being or not being a woman. The counsellor directed the client's thoughts to her own reasons for raising this and was able to work with Colleen on the difficulties that she was experiencing about her own body and the possibilities of her having children.

Boundaries need to be maintained, also, in the practical arrangements for the therapy hour. It is not helpful for the client to feel that he can control the ending of a session by introducing urgent material a few minutes before the finishing time. Children need to be reminded of the forthcoming ending, so that they can be ready to leave. There are very occasional instances when the counsellor needs to be more flexible. If a child is extremely upset and cannot recover by the end of the allotted time, the counsellor needs to be able to spend a few more minutes ensuring that the child can cope with meeting his escort or leaving the building. It may be advantageous, if a young person is distressed, for him to sit quietly for a few minutes to regain composure. In this case, if the counsellor is unable to check with the client, she should make arrangements for the situation to be monitored, so that she can receive the information as to when the client left. It is important that receptionists are able to handle such situations sensitively.

Supervision

When there is any ethical issue, the counsellor should first of all call upon her supervisor. A discussion of the matter can usually throw some light on the subject and the counsellor is not left alone with the problem. The supervisor should know if and when any other action needs to be taken. A children's counsellor therefore needs to be confident that the supervisor has knowledge of the law regarding children. The counsellor wants the supervisor to discuss the work with a view to enhancing her own skills and understanding more of the nature of children's traumas. Good supervision has an educative as well as formative element to it; professional development needs to be rounded by new learning and activity that will enable the counsellor to have more resources in her toolbox.

It is essential for the therapist to meet regularly with a supervisor who gives the therapist the time and space to get in touch with a metaview of the sessions. Talking over what was going on in the sessions and what communication the child might have given, together with an honest look at the emotions stirred up in the therapist, is an important part of the work. Without this check, the work could go on without in-depth thinking about the child client and the interactions between child and counsellor. To be therapeutic the relationship between the therapist and child has to be constantly re-evaluated to make sure that the child's needs are being met. Honest, open supervision gives an added safety measure for the counsellor, but more importantly for the client.

Summary

1. We explored some of the implications of working with children.
2. The Children Act 1989 gives guidance, and the counsellor needs to be aware of litigation issues.
3. If the counsellor–client relationships remain firmly within ethical guidelines, the counsellor should have confidence that her work stands up to scrutiny.
4. It is important to address confidentiality with the child client and also with referrers so that clear boundaries are maintained (as you proceed to look at the stages of counselling a child, the legal and ethical issues may become clearer).
5. Agencies have their own guidelines, of which counsellors working in these contexts should make themselves aware from the outset, so that they know how to proceed when situations arise. It is not helpful for counsellor or client to have a hiccough at a critical moment in the counselling relationship.

8

THE PROCESS OF
COUNSELLING A CHILD

Overview

In this chapter, we go through the stages of counselling, giving attention to working with the child client as an ongoing process. There are a number of vignettes, giving examples of how different children have negotiated various stages in the course of therapy. Beginnings and endings are of importance, but, as we will demonstrate, the main work is done in the middle phase of therapy.

Assessment

Assessment is a very important part of the process of counselling. It is the stage at which all parties need to agree the purpose of the counselling, the arrangements for the sessions and the responsibilities of each party. The person responsible for getting the child to the counselling room needs to act in the child's best interests. It is important to explain to the person who will be responsible for the child arriving that he/she recognizes the importance of a prompt start and makes this commitment to the child. Late arrival means that the child is not able to take the best advantage of the sessions. With an adult, the counsellor can use lateness to explore resistance or other reasons for lateness, but the younger child is dependent on an adult for escort and the child might well be agitated by the lateness. The feelings can be examined and the child empowered to ask the adult for more consideration regarding time, but the adult will not necessarily comply with the child's requests.

First of all the counsellor needs to decide whether the referred child will benefit from counselling. In a school situation, sometimes it is the head teacher or the special needs co-ordinator who selects the children. This can cause a problem, as the child might not benefit from the process, whereas the school's referral has been for the benefit of other children whose learning may have been disrupted by the referred child, or even for a teacher who has been exasperated by the child's continual presence in the group. There are sometimes difficult decisions for the counsellor to make in these circumstances, as it would be unethical to work with a child for whom it is unlikely there would be a beneficial outcome. Other people will sometimes argue that the child obviously needs help, but counselling is a relationship that requires the two parties to be able to communicate well with each other and there has to be a willingness on the part of the client to engage in the process voluntarily.

CASE EXAMPLE

Tommy

Tommy was brought to the counselling centre by his social worker, who wanted to negotiate some therapy sessions, saying that Tommy was unable to cope with his circumstances. Tommy was reluctant to speak to a counsellor and insisted that it was the social worker who needed help, not him. The social worker was present throughout the discussion. Tommy had been placed in a foster home after he had accused his father of sexual abuse. The young man admitted he had done this because he had a friend in foster care, who was having a very good time, whereas his parents were very strict with him and would not allow him to roam the town late at night. He had presented himself, at 13, to the social work office and asked to be taken into care. The social worker explained to him that there would have to be a good reason for taking him into care, such as being sexually abused within the family where he was living. Prompted by this, Tommy made allegations about his father. He was taken into care and lived with a foster family. His parents were heartbroken and felt they had no way to defend themselves. Although Tommy withdrew his statements later, by the time he did so, his parents felt that they could no longer control him. He was out on the town late at night, smoking and taking drugs. They wanted reconciliation, but saw no way forward.

Tommy sat in the chair, opposite his social worker, while the social worker explained how he wanted the family to sort out their problems; as a start, he wanted Tommy to have counselling. The counsellor was aware that Tommy was capable of understanding the process of counselling and he needed to want to come for sessions rather than being pushed into it by someone else. The counsellor suggested that Tommy should say what he felt about counselling. Tommy replied that he did not want to change anything in his life at present. The counsellor agreed that counselling would be unlikely to help Tommy if he was strongly against it, but it would give him the opportunity to speak with someone independent of the family situation about his feelings of the past few months and his desires for the future. Tommy said he would give it a go and attend four sessions. Tommy was quite adamant that he wanted to live his life in his chosen path. He felt a little sorry that he had caused his parents distress, but was determined that he was not going back to live with them. Having made his bid for independence, he was not going to give it up lightly. In the foster placement, he was able to do all the things that had been disallowed at home. He did say that he would be willing to talk to his parents.

Sadly, in the above example, the parents were unable to come to terms with how they had been treated. They wanted Tommy back, but felt that they would be unable to cope with his new lifestyle, of which they disapproved. Tommy could have continued in counselling for the sake of the social worker, but it would not have been for his own sake. The counsellor would have been colluding with the social worker to have offered more appointments. This would have made Tommy more indignant and perhaps put him off counselling for life! In the event, the counsellor had shown Tommy that his views mattered and that he was free to make his own decisions, although other people were affected by his choices. Counsellors can be all too easily drawn into the trap of feeling that they are required to take on clients who might benefit more from some other kind of help. Tommy's choices were not necessarily in his own best interests, but counselling would not have changed Tommy's mind.

Many children have many different needs, but it might not be the right time for counselling. Where there are a whole range of agencies involved with a child, there is often a parent or carer who is seeking solutions in any field possible. Often, it is better for the counsellor not to become yet another person on whom the child is foisted. Children can feel ostracized by having to attend clinics and special classes. To have another difference can be detrimental to their self-confidence.

There also has to be a clear reason for the referral and an idea of the underlying difficulties. If a child has experienced a known trauma, or where the child is unable to function within the normal limits of acceptability, there is cause for concern. The assessment process must look further to see if the child can communicate enough to make the counselling viable and whether the child has enough support to be able to attend the sessions regularly.

To assess a young child for counselling, it is necessary to have information from a parent or carer, as the child will be unable to commit to various parts of the contract. It is advisable to ensure that the child knows the reason for the assessment and is aware that he is the person whose concerns are pivotal to all that is being discussed. Play materials should be freely available and can be a great help in allowing the counsellor to see how the child interacts. But the playthings need to be in a place that brings the child into the group and not over in a corner of the room, which would allow the child to distance himself from the conversation. When a referrer wants to dominate the session, it is helpful for the counsellor to be able to relate directly to the child about his importance in the meeting.

At any assessment the needs of the child must be the focus. There are likely to be anxieties about the child and most of these will probably reside in the adults, but children do not need to be offered therapy because of the adult angst which surrounds them. The child needs to see the professional working with the parent/carer so that the child understands that therapy is not being imposed, nor is the child being 'handed over' to a professional, which would undermine the authority of the parent/carer. The offer of therapy is made to the child and described appropriately so that the child can understand what it is he will be doing.

CASE EXAMPLE

Quentin

Quentin was 12 years old when his mother felt that he would benefit from counselling. His school had noticed that he was over-sexualized in his behaviour towards male teachers and visitors to the school. Quentin was quite articulate at the assessment session and declared that he did not want any counselling. The therapist asked him if he had found it difficult to attend the session and he replied that he found it very easy to talk. The therapist asked if he would like the opportunity to talk to her on his own, having a session on a weekly basis. Quentin said that would be fine. When she explained that the centre offered counselling in that way with the option of using the materials in the room, Quentin was visibly relieved. He could not explain what he had previously thought counselling to be, but he thought something would be 'done to him' rather than him taking the initiative and using sessions for his own purposes.

Families are so often seeking a solution for the problems a child presents. There is a tendency to think that the counsellor will 'resolve' these problems and that in a few weeks they will have a child who no longer behaves in unsociable ways. The counsellor needs to explain that counselling is a process that enables the child to reflect on or play out inner worries; there may be times when the behaviours escalate as the child comes into contact with painful feelings. Referrers need to know that there are no speedy solutions and that the child will be offered time and space, but the counsellor will not be working to anybody's expectations. Therefore there are no guarantees about outcomes. It is very easy for parents to compare their own child with another child who may have received therapy. But they need to have it underlined that their child is unique and there are no answers to be presented.

Unless there is an understanding of the child's needs, then the counsellor has no way of thinking through what she needs to offer the child and how she needs to be in her interaction with the child. When a child is acting out, he needs an external person who will keep things safe both emotionally and physically. It is important the child can identify the counsellor and her room as a place of safety. When the child is feeling the inner pain and anguish, he needs to feel that the therapist is there beside him, willing to be in the painful situation. It is a matter of the therapist knowing what the child needs at each point of the process.

The assessment session will give the therapist clues about how the child will interact, how he will respond, how he will make use of materials. Questions can also be asked at the assessment. It is important that the child is given the first option of answering the questions and reference made to parents/carers only if the child asks them to help out.

Another important part of the assessment session is to give the child an understanding that the assessment is not the same as the ongoing counselling sessions. After the initial interview, the child will be only with the counsellor and the counsellor will not be telling anyone outside the room the content of the session unless there is a danger to the child. The referrers are there to give and gain information at the assessment, but once that has been done, the child will come into the room by himself and spend the hour with the counsellor.

Generally, the adolescent will attend by himself for the assessment. This is not always the case, as those who have not achieved autonomy will be dependent on an adult to present the state of affairs.

The first session

Although the counsellor will have met the child with referrers at the assessment, the first session with the child alone will take on a different complexion. This is where the relationship needs to begin. Each child will respond differently and the counsellor should have no set pattern with introductions; she needs to pick up the child's feelings about coming into the counselling room. Some children will feel at ease immediately and begin to explore. The counsellor can then be the onlooker until the child invites her participation. There are other children who may remain diffident and need some encouragement to explore the materials. With such encouragement, some children will find their way. Then there are children who will want to withdraw and may be frightened to be on their own. They may have fears of having been abandoned by the carers and left with a stranger. The child who appears to be nervous needs reassurance of why he has come, the use of the time, the assurance of the arrangements for collecting him and an acknowledgement of the feelings of nervousness. The child may then begin to communicate and the process of rapport can begin. There are some children who take a very long time to feel at all comfortable in the room. They may withdraw further and further from the counsellor; this is sometimes seen in a physical way, by the child getting as great a distance as possible between himself and the counsellor. The counsellor should not overwhelm the child with encouragement, but should allow the child the space and the counsellor should stay at a distance from the child, permitting him to feel unthreatened. The counsellor can begin to play with materials herself to model for the child that it is acceptable to use the materials. This sometimes encourages the child to venture nearer to see what is happening. Or the child might begin his own play at a distance. This is parallel play, and the child may need to get a sense of security in place before engaging with the counsellor. It is important to go at the child's pace and not try to hurry him into any communication that would put in jeopardy the fragile attempts to settle.

Children in new situations often have a sense of foreboding. Depending on their earlier lives, new places can be intimidating. Some children try to compensate for their feelings of apprehension by pretending that they do not care at all about coming into a new room with a new person. They may make a lot of noise and race about the room, not engaging with any of the materials, but quickly eyeing up all the possibilities. The counsellor can find this quite daunting (which is probably picking up the child's feelings), but should tolerate this behaviour and accept it as an expression of the child's unconscious fear of getting into any meaningful relationship. Ceaseless activity and/or ceaseless chatter make the child feel that he can control the situation, not letting anything happen that is outside that control. This could not go on for ever when the therapeutic alliance is established, but in the first session, it is desirable to allow the child to do whatever he normally would do in such a situation. The counsellor learns from this how the child defends himself and how precarious the ego might be.

During the first session, the child must be made aware of what is acceptable in the playroom and behaviour that will not be tolerated. It is easier to make the rules plain at the outset. Some counsellors prefer to give no restrictions until the child oversteps the mark, but often a child feels safer knowing the boundaries. These are very simple. A child should have access to all the materials in the room, unless there are private cupboards, which should then be locked. It is not wise to keep other children's work and special things in the playroom, as they could become the focus of another child's curiosity. The child is free to play in any way he chooses, except for hurting himself, hurting the therapist or damaging the property. It is also helpful to tell the child that the session takes place inside the room. If the child needs the toilet, he will be supervised to and from the toilet. This means that the child will not use the toilet as a means of escaping for part of the session and he will not be drawn away to other areas of interest. In particular, the child will not be able to interrupt other sessions that may be in progress.

When the boundaries are put in place, the child also needs to know what will happen if he infringes a rule. The session may have to be terminated if the child is putting himself or the counsellor in a dangerous position. If the sanction has been made clear, it is very important that when the child tests the boundary, it remains firm. The sanction needs to be carried out in a calm way, with a reiteration of the rule, the fact that it was broken, the fact of carrying out the sanction and the reminder that therapy can continue in the next session.

It is often said that first impressions are most important. With therapy the first session is the beginning of a new relationship. The counsellor needs to reflect on all that happens in the first session.

It is likely that the child will not begin to play spontaneously in the first session, but will explore materials to see what they are and what they will do. The objects, at this stage, are seen as objects. They will be examined rather than used.

It is important that the child uses the session for his own purposes, which means that the counsellor will not have an agenda for the child. One of the dangers for new counsellors is that anxiety can pervade the session. The counsellor feels that she should be doing something. If the counsellor enters the playroom with an agenda in mind, then the child is not free to express himself. He will sense the expectation or be guided by the counsellor's feelings towards the materials that will best please her. Children of a young age will often want to please the therapist. Troubled children have often survived by conforming to the demands of adults. The whole point of the therapeutic sessions is to have the child free from restrictions of external demands.

In thinking about the child's first session, and indeed, subsequent sessions, the counsellor can be left with feelings of not understanding what it was that the child was trying to convey. There is a great danger in jumping into interpreting the child's behaviour. The therapist needs to reflect on what was happening in the session and the feelings aroused both in the child and in herself. Reflection needs to be made about all the feelings that were in the room during the session: the feelings the child gave explicitly or implicitly and the feelings engendered in the therapist. To stay with the feelings and ponder them is better than trying to sort them out and make sense of them in the first instance. Staying with the not knowing is an important experience for the therapist. Adults want to know and like to tell themselves that they know, but in therapy, to see the world through the child's eyes is to not know. A child will be better served by the therapist staying with the not knowing. For trust to build, the child will need to work at his own pace and any premature intrusion into the child's world will diminish that trust.

Supervision is of great benefit when evaluating first sessions. Another very useful arena for the counsellor is the case discussion group, where a number of therapists meet to discuss case scenarios. Being able to describe a new client early in the process can be an immense advantage. It is helpful to get feedback from more than one person. Group supervision provides this forum and can provide different ways of dealing with the presented material that enables the counsellor to hear other people's views of what is happening in the counselling session. The counsellor can have the opportunity to role-play the child and this can be helpful, allowing the counsellor to get into the place of the child while others observe. This often allows the counsellor to understand more the feelings that the child may have experienced.

The child gives expression to his inner feelings through the medium of play; everything in the play has meaning. However, the therapist will not be able to find the meaning in the play at all times. The child is leading the session and will give the counsellor a great deal of information both through the play and verbally explaining why he is doing particular things. But there will always be those areas of play which the therapist cannot understand. Maybe the child is not understanding either. There is always the incommunicable bit of personality that remains hidden at the core of the self, which is not available to the conscious self. There are also unconscious drives which the child is expressing, without being able to identify them; this makes the play appear to be meaningless. The therapist has to remain with the meaninglessness. Bion talked about 'a letter Keats wrote to his brother in which he said it occurred to him what the great strength of Shakespeare was – he could tolerate mysteries and half-truths without an "irritable reaching for certainty"'.[44]

Memory is a very helpful tool for the therapist. Play episodes that appear to have no meaning can often come into the therapist's mind after the child has given other information in play. It is useful to, as it were, put things 'on the shelf' until such time as the activity can be looked at with hindsight and in the light of new material that the child is giving.

The middle phase

As the child becomes familiar with the materials, he will use them as props for his own purposes. These symbolic communications will, as Dockar-Drysdale notes, enable the child and counsellor to share:

> symbolic communication between a child and therapist is a way in which we can build up communication as we gradually come to understand the child's symbols. It is very rewarding to communicate in this way, and it will soon become clear what the symbols represent. There is a temptation to interpret at this juncture, and it is important to realize that once interpreted – however correctly – the symbols will be abandoned, so that, unless one is sure that the child is very near an understanding of his communication, it will bring an end to the slowly growing insight of both therapist and child.[45]

During the process of counselling, the playing child can often give more directly than the more sophisticated adult. Transference is often clearly handed to the counsellor. 'You be my mother', the child might request in a session. The child may then direct the counsellor to play out the part as his own mother would, which gives the counsellor insight into that relationship; or the child might want to try out a different kind of mothering.

CASE EXAMPLE

Hazel
Hazel was 13 when she attended counselling. She was a very small child for her age and had just started at secondary school. She told her counsellor that she wanted her to be her mother. Hazel gave all the instructions of how her

mother was to behave. She was to give Hazel everything she wanted. In the first few sessions the counsellor did as requested. When the relationship had become stable and Hazel trusted the counsellor, the counsellor decided that it was time to help Hazel tolerate some frustration. So instead of agreeing to everything Hazel requested, she suggested that Hazel would not always be able to have her own way. Hazel was quite angry about this and the counsellor was able to work with Hazel on the fact that the things which she demanded were not satisfying her and that she wanted something other than things. Hazel was able to talk about how her older sister had always tried to get her mother to stop Hazel from having any place in the home. The sister had made her look small; her feelings about this were all very raw at this time, as she was mixing with children at school who were much bigger than her physically and she was being teased about her diminutive size. Hazel's mother just laughed when Hazel complained. What she was wanting from her mother was assurance that her size did not diminish her as a person. In the transference, Hazel wanted to create a new mother who would give her what she wanted, but it took some time and the counsellor frustrating her 'wants' to get at the real issue of Hazel's feelings of being put down in the family group.

The transference changes from session to session. The counsellor needs to be what the child needs at each stage in the process. Sometimes, the child brings out in the counsellor many different feelings, not all of them positive. Workers in residential settings can feel intense negative emotions towards some children, who demand from them all the time. After a long working day, when a child becomes hostile and aggressive, patience can run out. Counsellors who use the counselling hour once a week are much less likely to feel as emotionally drained by a child, but there are still negative and ambivalent feelings that are bound to arise. Supervision is confidential and not part of the management structure so that such feelings can be discussed honestly and openly, without employment coming under question. There are many reasons why the counsellor might feel negative emotions. There is the countertransference, which can mean either the counsellor's own transference or the reaction of the counsellor to the child's transference. The counsellor may not want to be seen as the authority figure in the child's life and may resist the role that the child is needing to use.

Children often have a fear of abandonment and any alteration in the timing of his session may cause the child to fear that the therapist is about to leave him. This is especially true at times of breaks in the counselling. Although prior arrangements may have been made crystal clear, the child is feeling rather than thinking that the therapist is not going to return. Many of the children who are referred for therapy have had difficulties in relating to their primary attachment figures, who have been unreliable. Where this has happened the child will make an assumption that any adult with whom he makes an attachment will behave unreliably.

The therapist's reactions to the child need to be pondered too. Some children can draw out a response in the therapist that surprises the worker. This then needs to be measured to see if the reaction is from the therapist's own experiences of life or whether she is being given by the child the feelings that the child cannot tolerate. For instance, if a child begins to ask the therapist impossible riddles, the therapist can feel overwhelmed. If she had similar feelings back in her schooldays, when confronted by teachers asking seemingly impossible questions, the reaction might be the therapist's own anxieties reawakening. However, the child may want the therapist to feel how he feels about the things that are put before him from day to day, making the child feel that he cannot understand the situation and is at a loss to know how to respond.

The therapist's countertransference towards a child client needs to be thought about carefully. It would be all too easy for the therapist to want to repair damage the child had suffered at the hands of others. This is not possible. The therapist has to go through the bad experience with the child and help him to contain the devastation, but it is not helpful to the child to try to replace the past. The child may demand that the experience be changed, but this would lead to fantasies about the past rather than dealing with the real pain. It would amount to going around the difficult obstacle by taking a different path. What the child needs is for the counsellor to walk the same path, to share the anxiety and to give it back to the child as he is able to tolerate it. With child clients, there is more temptation to relieve the pain rather than to stay with it.

CASE EXAMPLE

Una

Several workers were being interviewed for a care post at a residential school for children who were severely emotionally distressed. At lunch, a 10-year-old girl blurted out, 'My Mum doesn't love me any more.' Una, one of the interviewees, immediately jumped in to reassure the child that she had got it all wrong; of course her mother loved her.

It had taken the child's therapist many months of work with the child to help her to understand that her mother had chosen not to see her any more. The child was coming to terms with the rejection. The visitor's comments undermined the reality of the situation, of which the child had more perception.

A child needs to know that the therapist does not need to protect herself from pain. Otherwise, the child will reverse the roles and take on the care of the therapist. There are occasions when the therapist will feel that the child feels frightened or panic-stricken. At such times, there is the temptation to find some kind of solution for the child or adolescent; for example, the therapist might be tempted to suggest ways which have helped her deal with difficult feelings. This immediately gives the child a warning that his feelings are too difficult to stay with; it is as if the therapist is holding up a placard saying, 'No further. Stop here.' Often, the therapist will find herself doing this when she becomes anxious about the content of the child's communication. The child will then be sensitive to the counsellor's anxiety and digress from the painful material or show frustration with the adult.

CASE EXAMPLE

Leah

Leah was 6 years old when her mother became very concerned. Leah had become aggressive and recently had attacked her grandmother in the car. Mrs C. realized that Leah had reason to be upset. Her grandfather had died about a year before and her schoolfriend's father had been killed in a road accident two months before she was brought to counselling. In her first session, Leah played with the toy cars, smashing them into one another and making a lot of noise. The counsellor could see the confusion and terror that the car crash had given to Leah. The little girl spoke of how she cried whenever either of her parents was going out in the car. From her friend's experience, Leah had believed that cars crash and kill the drivers. She was not afraid of going in the car with her parents, but could not tolerate the fear that her parents might not come back after leaving her. This separation anxiety was a regressive separation anxiety and it was easy to know the cause.

Leah began to play with animal puppets. She made the animals fight each other and the dog was always the victim of the other animals. The counsellor reflected back to Leah that the dog seemed to be the one which was set upon by the others. At the end of this session, Leah angrily turned on the counsellor, hissing, 'Don't you know you are supposed to be talking to me about my Granddad?' Quite taken aback by the hostility in this remark, the counsellor assured Leah that she could talk about her Granddad at any time and that in the next session they could start right there. Leah left.

In the next session, the counsellor reminded Leah of her request to talk about her Granddad; Leah proceeded to repeat the animal puppet play and to insist that the dog must be killed. Not understanding whether this had anything to do with Granddad, the counsellor suggested perhaps there was something that linked the dog and Granddad. Leah began to sob. She then told the counsellor how she had been told at school that when people die they come back as an animal, such as a dog. Every time she saw a dog, she wondered if it was her Granddad and she could not bear the thought that she could not recognize him, but he might be trying to communicate with her. The counsellor then asked Leah to tell what she thought had happened to her Granddad. Leah had Christian parents and she wanted to believe that Granddad had gone to a safe place. Giving Leah assurance that she could choose what she wanted to believe gave her the freedom to leave the reincarnational theory on one side. She began to calm herself and left the session very thoughtfully. Later in the week, Leah's mother left a message for the counsellor to say that Leah had changed, saying, 'I have got my daughter back.' After several more sessions, Leah expressed that she now did not worry about dogs and she was sure that Granddad was safe and not roaming the streets. Her hostility subsided and the counsellor planned an ending.

Projection and introjection are discussed in Chapter 3; they happen all the time. In counselling the counsellor needs to be aware of where things belong. A child client can easily see the world as a place full of opposites; there are good things and people, there are bad things and people. Ambivalence is difficult to manage and children take a long time to be able to give up the idea that a good mother can fail or that a neglecting mother can be caring in some ways. The young child keeps the good mother apart from the bad mother, accepting them as separate identities. The good mother feeds, comforts and enjoys the baby; the bad mother denies food, leaves the baby in discomfort and is tired of the baby, neglecting its needs. The splitting of the two, Melanie Klein described as the paranoid–schizoid position.[46] The baby may learn to tolerate good feelings about himself but not bad feelings, therefore these feelings have to be pushed out to somebody else. The reverse may be true; if the child has learnt that he is not valued, he may want to project all the good feelings out of himself towards others, confirming to himself that he is bad. This, of course, can continue into adulthood. Many clients in counselling come because of difficulties with ambivalence. There is a tendency in our culture to idealize and demonize, rather than seeing people as consisting of good and bad parts. This leads to wanting people, whose badness has been publicized, to be punished severely; this projection enables the spectators to feel that they are good while the punished are bad.

Thus it is often the case that the counsellor is given extreme feelings; she will be the good or bad object. Neither designation is satisfactory. To be 'good' is to conceal the reality of the counsellor's feelings, which are always mixed, but also to allow the child to experience a false way of being. To be 'bad' is to fail the child and to be made to feel that the work is of no value, of no consequence and to make the counsellor feel that she is useless. These feelings can indicate to the counsellor the way the child perceives himself and the defences that the child has had to build to prevent disaster in relationships.

For the baby, the mother gradually allows frustration, in order to allow the child to develop toleration of anxiety, but this has to be monitored by degrees so that the child does not reach the point of despair. In the same way, the counsellor has to go at the child's pace, meeting his needs in a safe way, but then giving back to the child the projected anxieties a little at a time, so that the child learns to own his own negative aspects as well as the good, or vice versa.

The counsellor has to be prepared to accept negative and positive projections. This is how the child manages life. He defends himself against the attributes which threaten to damage his personhood, or rather the perception that the child has formed of his own personhood. The counsellor needs to be aware that she may receive some of the projections more readily than others. There may be some that belong to the counsellor already and are therefore familiar. There may be others which the counsellor feels very unhappy at taking. The counsellor needs to remember that she is part of the process and that it is the client's needs that are to be addressed. Whatever feelings projections evoke in her are to be used for the understanding of the client's way of relating.

Counsellors sometimes become alarmed because they feel that child clients want to be dependent on them. It is only when a child can experience dependence that he can begin to separate. This assertion may seem paradoxical, but it is vitally important to accept. For most children this experience occurs in the early years of life; the dependent baby is cared for by its mother in a satisfactory way and then the mother is able to allow the baby the space to have his own existence, but with enough nurture for the world to be safe enough to negotiate. The child has to have the safe place from which to explore and to which to return if any danger threatens. Gradually the security becomes part of the child and the child is then able to hold the anxious times when mother is not present. As the child matures, the proximity of the caring figure is no longer necessary at all times. The child also learns that he can enjoy the presence of an adult for reasons other than having his needs met. Then there develops empathy and the ability to meet the other's needs, the recognition of the other's feelings, and there is a mutual relationship that perseveres throughout life. The disruption of the relationship at any point causes concern to both parties. Once an attachment bond has been made, separation and loss become difficult to bear. When separation and loss occur in the early part of a child's life it is devastating. The child has to go through the process of mourning, just as adults do, but the child often does not have the words or the understanding of rites which enable the adult to grieve satisfactorily.

If a child has not encountered a truly dependent state, he may want to invest in the counsellor. This will take a long time, as the child will not trust adults easily, having been let down in previous attempts. But there is a need for dependence as the basic bedrock from which to meet the world. It must never be the counsellor's intention to keep the child in a dependent relationship; but it is not to be glossed over as an unnecessary part of the process. This will bring about all kinds of feelings in the counsellor; to have a child dependent on the worker is draining.

Counsellors suffer a great deal of fearfulness about this. They tend to worry that they will be unable to move on with the child and that the child will become fixated upon them, or that the child will never get beyond the dependent phase. It is in the counsellor's remit to make sure that the process does continue and that the child's need for dependency is not extended beyond that time of necessity. However, to foreclose the stage prematurely would be to deny the child the new experience of dependence on which he could build a new way of relating to others. Children can be encouraged that they have lived through a new way of relating and that now they will be able to relate to other significant people differently. For the child who has had bad relations with family members, this can often be a way forward, providing the counsellor has allowed the dependent relationship and then allowed the relationship to move on, so that the child has moved from symbiosis to relating as a separate person. Children often feel that they want to re-create what they perceive the original symbiosis should have been. This is an impossible task and the child needs to let go of that image which is unreal and take up the real situation, using the selfhood that has developed during the therapy to build new relationships. It is more difficult for the child to build a new relationship with old partners than it is to encounter new people. Patterns have been established with previous significant figures and both sides have difficulty in making new contact patterns rather than regressing into the old script. It is necessary for the family to learn new behaviours and ways of being with the child if the child is to be allowed to relate differently. Blame cultures are often at the heart of family interactions. Where the child has been scapegoated as the source of family problems in the past, he will need the family to assume a new attitude. This means family members each taking their own share of problems without resorting to blaming the scapegoat. It is helpful for therapy to continue in the time that the child is making new approaches to family members. But there is the danger of the child playing the therapist off against family members. The family may feel that the child behaves differently with the therapist, so that she does not see the behaviours that the family has to manage. Splitting is easily taken on board. If the therapist has the opportunity to work with the whole family, so that interactions can be observed and commented upon, often the damage can be short-circuited. Other child members of the family have often grown up with the attitudes displayed by the adults and have become part of the blame culture with no recognition of what has been happening. They have assumed that the sibling has been the one with the problem and therefore the family has been unable to cope. When the child wants to change the pattern of his behaviour at home, there is great resistance. The rest of the family have a vested interest in the child fulfilling the role they have assigned to him. New patterns are uncomfortable and require a reorganization of attitudes and thinking.

CASE EXAMPLE

Barbara

Barbara was 11 years old when she was presented by her mother and stepfather for counselling. Her mother said that Barbara had always been a co-operative child until she remarried. Mrs D.'s 6-year-old son had welcomed the new husband and was 'as good as gold'. The new stepfather had an 11-year-old daughter and a 6-year-old son by a previous relationship. Three months previously the new couple had produced a baby of their own. Barbara was at loggerheads with her stepfather and her mother was finding it difficult to cope with her. Stepfather complained that Barbara would not listen to anything he said; he also felt that his wife always supported Barbara and did not support him in his attempts to discipline her daughter. The two girls and the two boys had had to share bedrooms when the couple started living together. This was a new experience for all of them. They also had half-siblings at school in their classes, where the mother's children had already established themselves. Now the new baby was to have a bedroom of her own.

The counsellor asked for a meeting with all the family as a way of understanding the dynamics of the situation. At the meeting, the younger children were very keen to say that Barbara was the one who caused all the trouble at home. She would not do as she was told; she did not do her homework (Barbara had a mild learning disability); she did not want to take her turn at washing the dishes. It was obvious that the siblings had picked up that Barbara was to take all the blame when things went wrong.

The fact that the other children were eager to say what was wrong with Barbara was evidence that they had already been immersed in thinking that this was the true picture. When the counsellor asked the children individually which members of the family got on well with other members, they all claimed to get on well with Barbara. They also thought that Barbara got on well with both her mother and stepfather. The counsellor realized that the only coupling that was not spoken about was that between the mother and stepfather. Suggesting that the children played with the toys, the counsellor asked the couple about their relationship. The mother immediately let down her defences and admitted that the new relationship was not working. She had had enough of her husband and it had been too difficult for her to face. The troubles had been easily concealed by her constant criticism of her husband's dealings with Barbara rather than facing the real issues.

But the other children had bought into this façade and believed it was true. Needless to say, the counsellor referred the couple for marital counselling and supported Barbara for a short time to adjust to the huge demands made upon her in sharing her home and school with a half-sister. It was difficult for the children to change their ways of behaving towards Barbara, as they too found it was easy to put blame on to her for their misdemeanours. The children copying the adult models.

Fairbairn wrote about the child moving from dependence to mature dependence.[47] He felt that the child should not be expected to move to independence, but he thought interdependence was a more comfortable term, allowing people to go on needing each other in all life's later years. Mature dependence requires the individual to recognize another's need as having equal value as one's own need, although the needs would be very different. For children who have not received adequate nurturing, the acknowledgement of another's need is outside their comprehension. They are like babies who are screaming to be fed; nothing can console them until they feel that someone is recognizing *their* need and giving to them the sustenance and comfort that shows concern. There is no capacity for anything else. So often, such children are not seen as expressing this enormous frustration, but as self-centred, manipulative children, who are deliberately causing difficulties for all those who try to deal with them. But many of their frustrations have never been met and the rage is still there. In therapy, the counsellor receives the rage and shows concern for the child who is being torn by the rage, and symbolically the counsellor has to see that the child is fed. This means meeting the child's basic needs; showing concern when the child is trying to destroy that concern; providing the reliable time and space so that the child knows that the counsellor will be there and reserve the space only for him. Once this is established – and it will take a long time for a child to believe that the counsellor has adequate concern – the child can then move from the screaming infant rage to the toleration of small anxieties, which the counsellor, just as the good mother, will make. The child then gradually learns that when things do not go according to his plan, the relationship still can carry on. Amends can be made and restitution is possible. For most children, these processes are dealt with in the first caring relationship, which meets all needs at first and then allows the child the space to feel frustration, but never to get to the point of despair, beyond which the relationship is irreconcilable. If despair is experienced, the process has to begin all over again, with the child beginning with mistrust and only building trust after repeated good experiences to counteract the awful feelings of despair.

Endings

The end of each session is a minor ending; the way each session ends can be a good model for working towards a good ending. There has to be some measure of clearing up when a child has finished his session. This is particularly the case if children follow one another in quick succession. A child coming into the playroom should find it ready to use. However, the counsellor does not want to stop a child from being messy and can suggest that the child might like to clear up. There are some children who enjoy clearing up and leaving the room as they found it; but there are a great many others who do not want to put things back. With these children, the session should end with enough time for the counsellor to rearrange the room.

It is good if the child clients can come and leave without seeing other users of the service. They will often ask the counsellor whether she sees other children. Their questions as to who they are and why they come can be given the reply that the child would not want other children to know that they come and for what purpose and that the counsellor always holds respect for each child. There can be unfortunate meetings if children are not collected promptly at the end of a session and it is important that the counsellor addresses this issue with the person responsible.

In all counselling, there is need for endings to be planned and for attention to be given to the process of finishing the therapeutic relationship. It is particularly important for children to have plenty of time to work with the ending processes. They need time to imagine what it will be like to be without the support that they have had. They need to rehearse how they will think through what to do with feelings that can be perceived as threatening. There has to be a degree of internalization of the relationship before this can be used by the child.

CASE EXAMPLE

Abi

Abi had been in counselling for nearly two years. The agency which made the referral discussed with the parents the possibility of Abi finishing her therapy. The counsellor requested that Abi be allowed to work with her until the Christmas holiday, giving a 12-week period in which to help Abi negotiate a good ending. When the counsellor first approached the subject, Abi protested that she needed to come for ever. It was her place and she wanted to hold on to it. The counsellor agreed with Abi that she felt her need was so great that she could not do without it, but that at some point Abi could feel that she had a new thing to do in her life and that she would want to let go of the playroom, although she could always keep it in her memory.

As the weeks went by, the counsellor referred to Christmas and that at that time there would be a break; she talked about how Abi had managed over the summer break. The termination of the counselling was mentioned in some way each week to give Abi the clear message that counselling was coming to an end.

At one session, Abi commented that she would miss her counsellor very much, but that she thought she would manage without her. The counsellor responded that it was a step forward for Abi to feel this way and encouraged her to think about how she now used the sessions compared with how she had used them when she first arrived. Week by week Abi and her counsellor went through some of the activities that Abi had enjoyed. It was as though she was asking for a mental scrapbook of the things she had dealt with and the ways she had found of being able to contain very difficult feelings. As she did this, Abi was strengthening her own containment and making sure that it would hold her. Abi then talked about her need to finish the counselling. In her young life, Abi had been abandoned on a number of occasions and the counsellor felt that Abi wanted to be in charge of this separation. She wanted Abi to feel that she could manage an ending in this relationship; she was not being abandoned. Abi had learnt to trust her; she had then weaned Abi enough for her to be able to grow enough ego strength to leave the counsellor herself. Abi found the last session difficult, but managed to talk about her feelings at leaving and to leave on time at the end of the session, saying appropriate goodbyes.

It is not always as easy as Abi's ending. For some children, therapy is prematurely ended either by parents or an agency that cannot commit to the contract agreed. This is very damaging for the child and has an impact on the counsellor. Where an ending is not planned, it often gives the child yet another experience of adults who promise something, but do not deliver the goods. The child is left feeling angry and hurt.

CASE EXAMPLE

Zac

Zac was 14 when his social worker decided that the only way he could stay in his foster family was if he agreed to attend counselling sessions. Zac was a very angry young man; he had been taken into care when he was quite small and had had several foster placements. He arrived for his first counselling session breathing out venomous threats towards everyone. He did not want counselling and he was feeling punished by his foster parents and his social worker. He had taken to running away from school, so that he could get away from everyone. On a number of occasions Zac had not been found until late at night. He was causing everyone consternation. The counsellor talked with Zac about his feelings of anger towards all those who were making decisions for him. He realized that Zac would see the counsellor as yet another person interfering with his life. The counsellor admitted how he felt and Zac began to calm down. The counsellor explained that he would not tell Zac that he had to come for counselling, nor would he accept anybody else making that decision other than Zac. The counsellor was willing to give Zac a regular appointment, but only on the grounds that it was Zac who requested it for himself. The counsellor did not want Zac to agree then and there, but gave Zac his card and said that if Zac wanted an appointment, then he could telephone the counsellor himself to make an appointment and if that appointment was made, then they would discuss their frequency of meetings and the contract would be with Zac himself. The social worker was very concerned that the counsellor was unwilling to engage with Zac on her directive, as she felt she needed to take control of this boy's life. Zac did telephone the counsellor and agreed to four meetings, during which he was able to explore how his views and wishes were never heard; there were a number of people who said what would happen to him.

Zac was an adolescent and was having the struggle that every adolescent faces. But he was not able to negotiate with significant people, as there had been so many changes in his life structure and significant relationships had come and gone frequently. He had no base from which to make a bid for his independence. His rage was infantile, because his infant life had been unpredictable and his rage never contained by a safe carer. Every time he began a new relationship it was aborted by his being moved on to new carers. Zac felt he could only trust himself, yet he did not know who he was. He was a desperate young man, but long-term counselling at that time would have been for him to have made a bid to remain the child in the relationship. As an adolescent, this would have been tantamount to selling out to the adult world, rather than finding his own competencies.

Many adolescents want their street credibility and therefore may deal with a specific problem at a short burst of therapy, but cannot afford to engage in long-term work that would confuse their volatile emotions even more. This is true of most adolescents, but young women sometimes find it helpful to engage in long-term work, particularly those who are bereaved of their mothers in earlier life. It seems as if they want to know about their mothers and what caused their deaths. They want to identify with a real person. Quite often, when a mother has died when the girl was small, she has been given childish information about her parent, but never liked to ask about the truth. When she reaches adolescence, she often wants to know what her mother was like when she was young. Where grandparents survive, they can be a great help to the adolescent girl in giving detailed descriptions of the dead parent, making the child realize the reality of her personhood.

CASE EXAMPLE

Anita

Anita was 17 when she asked for counselling. She was thinking of leaving home and going to art college. She was not getting on at all well with her father. Her stepmother was trying desperately to 'mother' Anita, but Anita was unwilling to be civil in the home and she ignored any requests. Her parents were afraid that she would soon be in trouble with the law, as she had taken to drinking heavily and was tempted by the drug scene. The counsellor found it difficult to connect with Anita, as she displayed the same disinterest in the counselling sessions. But Anita said she wanted to continue. It was a place 'out of earshot' of her nagging parents.

After many months, Anita spoke of being unsure of her sexuality; this troubled her. At the following session, Anita disclosed that she had been told that her mother had died of cancer, but in reality she thought her parents had split up and her mother had gone abroad. Each day she imagined that there would be a knock at the door and it would be her mother returning to find her. This longing was interfering with Anita's life. The counsellor talked to Anita about asking her father for more information about her mother. It was obvious that Anita had never had real conversations with her father, as any mention of her mother made him extremely upset. Anita's grandparents were alive and soon Anita was visiting them regularly and they agreed to furnish her with any information they could. Anita came to her counselling sessions with vigour and full of the facts she was discovering. There had been a part of her that had been dead with her mother, yet had not accepted that her mother had died. So she had been living in a kind of limbo. Anita's grandparents then revealed that they had a video of her mother when she was young. Anita was able to discuss with the counsellor all her mixed emotions about wanting to view the video, yet not knowing whether she would be able to contain all the feelings that would well up within her. Anita decided to watch the video with her grandparents. She found the experience deeply moving in many ways. She found that she now could believe that she had had a mother and that her mother was a real person, all of which she had doubted without being able to put it into words. She delighted in wanting to be female and feminine. Her great longing then was to ask her father to watch the video with her, so that she would know that they shared this knowledge of her mother. Sadly, while Anita was in therapy, her father was unable to agree to watching the video with his daughter. He felt that it would raise too much sadness for him and he was unwilling for that sadness to be put on display in front of Anita.

The counsellor was aware that ending with Anita would be another painful experience. But Anita had the support of her grandparents and they would continue to talk with her about her mother. Anita now knew that she wanted to be female, whereas before she had been uncertain. She became a real part of her family; she worked at school in order to get qualifications to enter college. Because the counsellor was able to point to so many new beginnings in Anita's life, Anita was able to contain the feelings of ending with appropriate sadness.

Younger children often want to take something away from the playroom with them. This is not a good idea if the rule has always been that the playroom items remain in the room. To allow a child to take something from the room is like allowing the child to be delinquent because of the ending. A photograph of the playroom could be appropriate. This might bridge the therapy sessions and the child's own internal picture of the sessions. Working with taking away what has been happening in the playroom is a good focus for endings. The child suggesting how the ending might be marked is also helpful. The child then prepares for the ending with the counsellor and it is not an imposition.

After therapy, a child should not be encouraged to keep in contact with the therapist. An ending needs to be completed. Where counselling takes place in schools, the ending of the therapy should mean that the therapist does not seek information about children or ask about past clients in a way that infringes the child's confidence.

Where endings are managed well, the child can learn a great deal. So many children have experienced bad endings, but now there is the opportunity for the therapist to make the ending of therapy a new way of working at endings. Children who have been let down so often want to avoid endings, but it is part of the fabric of life. To empower them to be able to leave a situation well and to feel part of the ending is a valuable lesson. Just as the mother cannot go on with the child in the same relationship, the therapist has to be working towards a maturing of both self and the child during the therapy leading up to ending on a positive note. The therapist has to let the child down at some point during the work, but it should not feel to the child as though the termination of therapy is the first point at which the therapist has allowed any disappointment. The best can be made of breaks in the therapy. The child will express anger, but it is therapeutic that he experience small let-downs over a period of time. The expressed anger can be worked with, acknowledged and processed with the counsellor. Anger does not destroy the relationship but deepens it. Both child and therapist can survive difficulties and still work on. There is disruption but with negative and positive gains, all of which can be held. These experiences worked through within the relationship give a new foundation for the future working through of dilemmas rather than giving up on relationships with the assumption that a disruption or ending in some way depletes the person and renders the child incapable of sustaining relationships.

Counsellors often feel insecure about when to finish the counselling sessions with a child. As we have seen, the ending needs plenty of preparation and discussion. There is a role for supervision that helps the counsellor to work through her own feelings about endings. Having worked with a child over a long period of time, the counsellor will also feel that the child might perceive the ending as being another rejection. The counsellor needs to focus on the child's process, but in order to do this adequately it might be necessary for the counsellor to process her own feelings about the ending away from the child. Supervision provides the time and space for the counsellor to reflect on the real feelings and the transference feelings which have been apparent in the work.

Where the child moves on from a planned ending, the therapist is generally feeling that the work has been satisfactory. When decisions are made to stop therapy prematurely, for lack of finances or resources, the therapist can feel anger that the child's needs are not uppermost in the minds of decision makers. With the hostility that the child might show towards the therapist for abandonment, finding the best way to handle the cocktail of feelings needs careful thought. It is helpful for the therapist to be able to conclude the work with the child by making closure with a supervisor of the case, giving time to any emotions that have been aroused in the final sessions.

Summary

1. We looked at the structure of therapy and saw examples illustrating each of the stages, and we saw that counselling a child is a process over time.
2. The first and last counselling sessions have particular significance.
3. The therapist and child work together within the therapeutic alliance.
4. Therapy is a distinctive activity which gives unusual time and space for focus on specific issues.
5. It is important to remember that children operate generally in a much wider context, so therapy must take account of the other spheres in which they have to operate. This is discussed in the final chapter.

9

THE CHILD IN CONTEXT

Overview

It is very important that we do not forget that the child client is part of a wider social world. Outside the therapy room, he has to navigate his way through various other situations. There is the family setting, often school and constellations of relatives and friends, each situation demanding that the child interacts. The aim of this chapter is to recognize some of the issues that can occur for the client in the rest of his week and to demonstrate how knowledge of these can help those who work with groups of children to better understand a few of the dynamics which occur in the process of group work.

Systems

Systems theory was popular in the 1970s and has been developed in different ways. It was used particularly in the residential care of children (see Ward 1993[48]), and in family therapy (see Bruggen and O'Brian 1987[49]). But systems thinking is helpful to any worker or therapist because of the importance of the context of the child, which has to be held in mind, though the worker has only the child with whom to bring about change. However, each change in the child will influence his other relationships and if the changes cannot be integrated, it is important that the therapist keeps in mind the wider picture of the child's life, and protects against the child being put in situations that prove more difficult.

No child lives in isolation. He is part of other systems, for example his educational context, his friendship groups, clubs in and out of school to which he belongs. All of these systems change over time: school classes change, young people move in and out of clubs and friendships switch quite frequently. The family is the primary social group into which individuals are born and upon which they initially depend for nurture and for the physical and psychological protection offered by intimate relationships. This may be any one of a number of patterns and over the child's maturing years, the shape of the family may change any number of times.

The family is a system itself; it is affected by other systems from outside itself, known as supra-systems, and it has subsystems within it

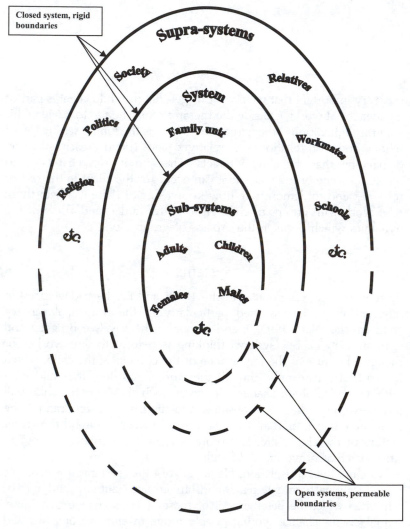

Figure 3 Systems

(see Figure 3). It is a process of change within a structure. There are open systems in families and closed systems. In the closed systems, there may also be enmeshed families. These families are those where the family members are co-dependent upon each other and cannot separate as individuals. This may happen between all the family parts or there may be a pairing which operates within the family, with other members more open to the outside world. Of course, the extremes of open and closed systems are rarely, if ever, seen. There are a whole host of constellations and they are changing all the time. Occasionally, open family systems can be extreme to the extent that the children involved cannot distinguish who is within the family unit and who is outside it.

CASE EXAMPLE

Poppy

Poppy was unable to say how many people were in her family, nor could she choose dolls to represent it; she knew her mother, an aunt and her grandmother. Beyond that she had no idea as to whether any of the men who came and went were part of the family. This was compounded by the fact that the three women were so enmeshed that they were unable to separate. Poppy described how she and the three women rotated sleeping arrangements in the three different homes. Though the women were enmeshed, the system for the men coming and going was too fluid, which made Poppy anxious and confused. There were occasions when the rotation was not possible and Poppy felt that she wanted to know where she would be sleeping at night.

Within closed systems, there are likely to be rules, roles and secrets that are held firmly, but not allowed discussion. These things grow within the family group and the members are aware of their obligations, though there is no directive. This often goes from one generation to another.

There needs to be a balance, where the family interacts within itself, but with boundaries that can provide a filter for interrelating with others outside. It is a coming and going, making connections, giving and taking. If this does not happen, emotional flourishing is compromised.

Working with families is a specialized area of work. Usually, a family therapist engages with all the members of the family. But there are times when the counsellor might feel that it is helpful to see other family members to understand the dynamics of the system in which the child is living, to recognize the context in which the child is maturing. The influences on the child need to be understood; the only way the therapist can understand is to listen to the stories and to check out the meanings that the family members attach to the narratives.

There are creative ways of using the family session. If the counsellor shows the family into the counselling room, it is of interest to see how the seating is taken or allocated. The family can be given a task to work on together. Large sheets of paper can be used for them to draw something. It is very revealing to the counsellor to see how the family set about such a task. There are times when nothing is put on to the paper, because nobody can agree what should be produced or they argue about the means of getting it done. The best thing is for the counsellor to observe the family interactions and to say as little as possible. However, there are times when intervention is necessary. If one member of the family describes a problem, it is not enough to take for granted that the story has been told. It is one person's perception of the situation. It is good to check out with the rest of the family how each member sees the issue being discussed.

The technique of *circular questioning* is a useful tool. When one member of the family declares how another behaves or reacts, a checking-out with that person helps to clarify; each family member should be able to describe how he or she sees the issue. For many families, it is the first opportunity they have had of sitting down calmly with each other to really look at what is happening in the family group. Sometimes there are surprises for people; they had no idea that another family member thought about things in the way described. At home, things are sometimes said and done in the heat of the moment and there is no time for reflection. If the temperature of the discussion rises, the counsellor can suggest that nobody speaks for a few moments, but that everyone sits quietly and thinks about what is happening. It is vital that each family member speaks for him or herself. The use of 'they' and 'we' needs to be checked and the speaker made to own the feelings spoken, without assuming that others feel or think in the same way. The counsellor needs to discover the location of the anxiety – who is it who is anxious, and about what? It may be a specific event that has triggered a crisis or it may be an ongoing family dilemma. Containing the anxiety in some way is essential. This can be approached by letting the family members who feel anxious describe their anxieties. Their coping skills in previous situations may help them to face this anxiety more confidently. Frequently, family members have extrapolated from the real situation, worried about what will happen 'if' the problem worsens. Fears about the future often originate in past events, and if the family can recognize the link and understand that it is defending itself 'in case' a similar event should occur, it can lower the levels of anxiety.

Another way of helping the family members to talk about an issue is *reframing*. The therapist suggests that the problem facing the family does not have to be seen only in one way. Many families have talked around a problem, becoming more and more stuck because they have seen it from one perspective only.

CASE EXAMPLE

Pauline

Pauline was in her final year of compulsory schooling and she wanted to be a hairdresser. Her parents both wanted Pauline to go to university and were horrified by Pauline's repeated requests to leave school that year. Because no progress could be made by seeing Pauline on her own, the family came for a session. Her father set out his disappointment with his daughter and the fact that she was throwing away her education. Her mother bemoaned the fact that her daughter was a bright girl and could do anything. For her, hairdressing was below the expectations she had for Pauline.

The therapist suggested that Pauline should look at the disadvantages of her leaving school and that her parents should think about the advantages that might come to the family if she left school. To their surprise, Pauline's parents discovered that they liked the idea of her being financially independent before they had expected; they would have a daughter who would have other things to think about and felt she would be a happier person with whom to live. Pauline understood that her parents were somewhat disappointed and wondered whether if she did a college course in hairdressing, her parents would feel happier.

In this way, the family was open to new ways of thinking of its problem. The conversation changed from the entrenched arguments to animated discussion as to the different ways parents and daughter could look at this matter. They had reframed the problem and had opened out more possibilities for a way forward.

Overlapping systems are created when families reconstitute. It takes time for different systems to synchronize. Stepfamilies have particular problems with which to contend. Before the families come together, the wicked stepmother may have been an image conjured up in the new female partner and in children's minds. Adults may well be in love with each other and assume that their children will love the partner and accept new siblings. They are sometimes told that they just have to accept a ready-made package. There is no opportunity to grow with the family as in first families. Frequently, people describe how the dynamics change between husband and wife when a child is present. One big mistake is for step-parents to believe that they can replace the natural parent. It is much healthier for all concerned if the new parent is prepared to let the stepchild grieve for the loss of his first parent, or make a firm commitment to respect the child's contact with his biological parent and not intrude upon this process. Where a child has lost a parent through death, the child needs to feel the space left by the lost adult; there may have been special activities that are lost. It is better to leave the space, than to try to fill it with someone else. It is all too easy for the parent, anxious to forge a good relationship between a new partner and the children, to assume things are going well. This may extend even to the point of telling the children that they are glad it is all right when, in reality, the children may be suffering deep anguish and grief and are angry about the whole situation. The therapist can offer the space for the child to explore all the emotions surrounding the issues of sharing his parent with someone else and having to share with other children coming into the household or his entry into someone else's household.

Groups

Any group is a system, which incorporates its individual members. When constituting a group of children, each one comes from his own unique background. It is not easy, especially in the early stages, to contain all the individual needs in order for the group identity to come into being.

Working with children in groups can be a useful way of giving children, who are experiencing similar problems, the experience of meeting other children who are going through comparable difficulties. This is not group therapy, which is a very specific skill and requires an experienced psychotherapist. Such a group is designed to allow the participants to deal with issues that arise from the members and to then process those issues and their effects on individuals and the group; there is no agenda. A facilitator will help in the processing of the material, but will not participate as a group member. Group work tends to have leadership and structures that direct the group. Such work can have therapeutic benefit for the group members, although a group cannot meet individual needs in the same way as one-to-one sessions can.

There are so many children needing help and one way in which more needs may be addressed is by group work. The assessment of a child for working in a group needs to be carefully carried out. If the child needs individual therapy, it is unlikely that a group will be able to contain that child.

Group work has to have a focus to make it safe enough to be of value to the participants. There has to be planning, rather than the non-directive techniques used with the individual child client.

The group members have to have something in common in order to form a group with a purpose. Usually groups are formed to deal with a particular dilemma, e.g. children who have lost a parent; children who are living with a drug abuser; children who have been fostered.

There need to be some rules that the children can share for the safety and well-being of each member. These can be decided democratically and in a positive way. The rules for each group will be diverse as the mix of adults and children will be different. They should be agreed with the group at the outset of meetings. This enables each child to be reassured as to the limits on behaviour. Sanctions should be clearly stated and not left until the child oversteps the limits. Group needs must be held in priority over individual needs. If there is a child who constantly needs individual time, then it is dubious whether the child should remain in the group. It is useful to have other resources, so that the child who cannot cope within the group can be redirected into personal help.

Some counsellors find it difficult to work with groups because they try to apply individual techniques. The whole point of a group is to share a common theme. If there are six children in a group and the group is non-directive, then there will be six themes. To select members of a group, there has to be a decision as to what the group intends to provide. If there is to be any therapeutic value, there has to be an overall aim for the group and component activities that make it possible for the children to express themselves in a way that will achieve its purpose. It is making a safe framework within which the children will feel secure enough to share.

The leadership of any group needs to be well planned. There will need to be an understanding among the group members as to how the leadership functions. There can be a main leader, with two assistants, or there can be co-leaders (often beneficial to have one of each sex), with an assistant, or three generic co-leaders.

Leaders need to decide whether a group aims to be therapeutic or educative. Of course, it can be both, but the therapeutic value means that the children have to be able to voice and/or act out some of their internal world.

Three adults is the minimum number for a children's group. If a child needs to be taken out of the group for any reason, there are two other adults to carry on the activities. Otherwise, one child's need may sabotage the whole group process. There will be times when a child's emotions become too difficult to hold in the group and individual attention may allow emotional first-aid to be rendered and the child then to re-enter the group.

There is no alternative to good preparation. Group workers should plan together, so that they are agreed on their objectives and the way in which the group will proceed. Expectations give children a sense of what is required of them in the group. Leaders often get what they expect; if leaders go anticipating there will be difficult behaviours they are likely to transmit their apprehension to the children, who will act it out.

The child who has been a victim may perceive the group as persecutory, although the other members of the group may have no idea that the victim member has such a perception. He may try out the group to have the feelings either confirmed or discredited.

If the group becomes cohesive, there will be all kinds of feelings if a member leaves or is absent without having given a reason. The group may feel that it has let the person down, or there may be a fantasy that the person has taken either the good things or the bad things out of the group. It is likely that another group member will take on a role that the absent member may have taken away. Leaders sometimes request that a group member be removed, only to find that another child is taking on the behaviours of the removed child. Leaders can also discover other problems when they think they have dealt with the hindrance!

Another phenomenon that occurs in the group is pairing. An alliance occurs which the rest of the group encourage, though not consciously. The pairing may be to criticize the group, or it may be to connect with each other, or it may be disruptive. In any case, the group members look to that pair to play out some of their disowned feelings.

All the members or the group will be trying to mould the shape of the group to match their own needs. The members will expect the adult to help them to find ways of meeting these needs, but also the needs of the other group members. Children in groups will want to know where the boundaries lie. They will test out whether the group is safe. For example, if children are told that unacceptable behaviours within the group will receive one warning and a second misbehaviour will mean that the child must leave the group for a certain amount of time, the rule needs to be enforced at the first instance. Otherwise, the other group members will feel that the group is too vulnerable and that the children will be able to run riot. There are many instances of counsellors wanting to make an exception for a child – with good reason – but thinking only of the individual need rather than the need of the group to be held in a secure environment. In supervision, counsellors argue that the child in question needed special leniency because of a prevailing difficulty. But the group has then deteriorated into merely a holding operation. Other children resort to bad behaviour and it is not then possible to enforce the rule.

There are levels of stress which can be tolerated by some leaders, which would be unacceptable to others.

CASE EXAMPLE

Group A
An art therapist and a counsellor ran a group for six children affected by drugs within their families. They planned activities for the children, set the rules with the help of the children and allowed choosing by the children within prepared activities. There were some challenges to authority, and when individual needs became too difficult for the group, one of the adults took the child aside, while the other managed the group.

From this experience, the leaders looked at the way things felt and decided that the group was hindered when left with only one leader, so brought in more help.

CASE EXAMPLE

Group B
A similar group, with new leaders, was structured in every detail. The children were set tasks, and although contributing answers to some questions, they were rigidly controlled. The leaders were unable to discuss the group without feeling that challenge would undermine their authority. They absented themselves from supervision sessions.

In the former group, there was openness to learning on the part of the leaders; in the second group, there was a defence against the leaders' own stress. The leaders could not allow the children and their emotions to have space for fear that the group might erupt. It functioned well as an educative group, but could not be described as therapeutic. In the first group, the stress of the children was acknowledged sympathetically; in the latter it was not allowed to be voiced.

The children in the first group felt sadness when the group came to an end – a very appropriate response. The second group left without the expression of feelings. They wrote about the things they had discussed in the group in a factual way, and they were more able than the children in the first group to write what they had learned in an objective way. Theoretical knowledge can become a stumbling block. The experience that children need from group leaders is a real meeting with them. Counsellors often believe that professionalism will be best served by remaining completely calm and unaffected by what is communicated to them. There is a vast difference between not being shocked by what children say and do and acknowledging the feelings that the child can arouse in the counsellor. Working with needy children is stressful and unless that stress is communicated, then the counsellor is likely to put up defences or to burn out. The communication of the stress should be addressed in supervision. Where the counsellor has a relationship with the supervisor that has built total honesty, there will be the admission of anger, hate and all the negative emotions along with the positive. With a place of safety to deposit these feelings, the counsellor will be able to continue to be available to the children for the depositing of their negative as well as positive emotions.

Leadership of a group demands different skills from counselling individuals. Leaders have to work together and share common goals; this cannot be left to chance. The first time group leaders come together, they need to know how they will work with each other and how they will resolve any differences. The group has to be able to rely on the adults giving, as closely as possible, the same containment and care to each member. It is good for leaders to work with different children in the group; otherwise there is a tendency for competition to rise between sub-groups and between the leaders.

CASE EXAMPLE

Group C
Two leaders took on a student to help with leading a group. Difficulties soon arose and the supervisor of the project suggested that the three meet with her to discuss the situation. The student felt unwelcome and that he was being treated by one of the others as an underling. He described how he had no problems at all with the other leader. He held one as 'bad' and the other as 'good'. The leader who received the positive feedback did not recognize the splitting and preened herself, while the one receiving negative feedback refused to take any of the comments on board. The supervisor reminded all three of the splitting process that was going on.

Leaders will not be good at picking up the children's trying to break their partnerships if they cannot work with their own processes. After a group, the leaders need to debrief; this can feel like hard work at the end of a session, but if it is not done immediately after the group, much of the information will be forgotten.

Evaluation is essential to consider whether the aims of the group are being met. The individual needs that have arisen can be discussed. The review should be taking a critical look at what happened, in the group, not in order to disapprove, but in order to have creative confrontation of the things that happened, and might be handled in a more appropriate way. This is the learning experience. There has to be the understanding that everything can be discussed. Counsellors should never feel that they know the way things should be done. Each scenario is different. Discussion should bring out all the hypotheses and be used to sift through ideas. It is a great pity when leaders feel demeaned if anything is questioned, rather than having a robust attitude that wants to further knowledge and insight by probing the facts and feelings.

CASE EXAMPLE

Shona
Shona worked with groups in a residential situation. She was very dedicated to her work, which she found demanding. Shona worked with the children effectively and was always quick to comment on incidents that arose. When she was upset by the violence or threats that children made, she found it very difficult to reflect on it. Instead, she would become very emotional herself and take on the victim role, suggesting that she had tried her best and now everyone else was criticizing her. She would then challenge people to do the job as well as she did it. She often left the group in tears, so did not take part in further discussion.

Shona was unable to question her own practice for fear of being seen as a failure. Her colleagues valued her work and were not criticizing her abilities. They shared with her how they often felt at their wits' ends in dealing with the difficult behaviours. But Shona then felt that she was the 'good' worker and they could be put in the 'bad' role. Thus she was splitting, and though her supervisor tried to help her understand these phenomena, she was unable to process her feelings. It was not long before Shona resigned.

When a group is working effectively, the experience of the members should grow emotionally and socially in their meeting with others. It can be a very valuable encounter.

In the emotionally fluid atmosphere of the group the children discover new dimensions to their own personalities. . . .

. . . Each member of the group holds a memory since each and every person's feelings and behaviours within the group must have an impact on everyone else. Each event becomes inextricably woven in to the fabric of that group's experience and memory.[50]

Summary

1. We took a brief look at systems theory in order to recognize the systems outside therapy in which children operate.
2. Children are always a part of other systems – which are affected by supra-systems and may contain any number of sub-systems.
3. The counsellor needs to be aware of the influences in children's lives and to understand how any change in the children will affect the system.
4. It is sometimes possible to bring together children from different systems into a group. Therapeutic work can be achieved by careful planning, implementation and evaluation, but it is a very different structure from the individual work with one child.

Conclusion

Working with children in therapy presents many challenges. We never can tell what will be required of us when we join a child on his journey. There will be roles to play, tasks to be accomplished and, most of all, undivided attention to be given. As soon as the child is able to contain himself, we say goodbye to him. It is unlikely that we shall know of his future success or failure. But for the brief time in his life that we travel with him, we try to give him the most facilitating setting in which he can explore his inner and outer worlds. The child, who has experienced pain and trauma in his earliest years, may heal. He may always carry the scars, but be able to bear the scars without the crippling effects of unresolved pain. Early intervention can bring release, allowing the true self to find its place in the community to which it belongs. Therapy is an adventure worth pursuing. All who embark upon it will find themselves opening up in a new way both inwardly and outwardly. Working with children enables the therapist to discover herself in innovative and fresh ways. It is not that the therapist only gives to the child; there is much to receive as well. Above all, the therapist has to remain intact, a person in her own right, who keeps her own counsel. Barbara Dockar-Drysdale reminded all those who came into contact with children who need emotional help that they should aim to have 'Something to give, something to take and something to keep'.

REFERENCES

Chapter 1

1   *www.teachernet.gov.uk/wholeschool/sen/ypmentalhealth/factsand_figs/* © Crown Copyright.

2   D. Stern, *The First Relationship: Infant and Mother* (Harvard University Press, 2004).

3   D. Winnicott, *The Child, the Family and the Outside World* (Penguin, 1991).

4   J. Bowlby, *Attachment and Loss: Vol. 1: Attachment* (Pimlico, 1997).

5   T. Brazelton & B. Cramer, *The Earliest Relationship: Parents, Infants and the Drama of Early Attachment* (Karnac, 1991).

6   L. Gomez, 'Humanistic or psychodynamic – What is the difference and do we have a choice?', *Self & Society* 31(6) (Feb./Mar. 2004).

Chapter 2

7   A. Piontelli, *From Fetus to Child: an Observational and Psychoanalytic Study* (New Library of Psychoanalysis) (Routledge, 1992), p. 34.

8   L. Hopper, 'Communication between Mothers and Fetuses' (thesis, University of Reading, 1993).

9   Ibid.

10 D. Winnicott, *Through Paediatrics to Psychoanalysis: Collected Papers* (Brunner-Routledge, 1992).

11 Piontelli, *From Fetus to Child*.

12 T. Verny & J. Kelly, *The Secret Life of the Unborn Child* (Times Warner Paperbacks, 1988).

13 Winnicott, *The Child, the Family and the Outside World*, p. 88.

14 D. Winnicott, *The Maturational Processes and the Facilitating Environment* (Maresfield Library) (Karnac, 1990).

15 A. Sansone, *Mothers, Babies and Their Body Language* (Karnac, 2004) and Stern, *The First Relationship*.

16 E. Erikson, *Childhood and Society* (Vintage, 1995).

17 J. Bowlby, *A Secure Base* (Routledge, 1988).

18 Winnicott, *The Maturational Processes and the Facilitating Environment*, p. 100.

19 M. Lanyado, *The Presence of the Therapist: Treating Childhood Trauma* (Brunner-Routledge, 2004), pp. 123–4.

Chapter 3

20 B. Dockar-Drysdale, *Therapy and Consultation in Child Care* (Free Association Books, 1993), p. 96.

21 L. Spurling, *An Introduction to Psychodynamic Counselling* (Basic Texts in Counselling & Psychotherapy) (Palgrave Macmillan, 2004), p. 21.

22 Dockar-Drysdale, *Therapy and Consultation in Child Care*, p. 104.

23 B. Dockar-Drysdale, *The Provision of Primary Experience: Winnicottian Work with Children and Adolescents* (Free Association Books, 1990), p. 75.

24 M. Hunter, *Psychotherapy with Young People in Care: Lost and Found* (Brunner-Routledge, 2001), p. 162.

25 A. Lester, *The Angry Christian A Theology for Care and Counselling* (Westminster John Knox Press, 2003), pp. 195–6.

26 The Samaritans, *Key Facts: Young People and Suicide* (Ewell: The Samaritans, 2001).

27 N. Parker, 'Eating disorders', pp. 387–404 in M. Lanyado & A. Horne (eds), *The Handbook of Child and Adolescent Psychotherapy* (Routledge, 2000), pp. 393–4.

Chapter 4

28 D. Winnicott, *Playing and Reality* (Routledge, 1996), p. 53.

29 Piontelli, *From Fetus to Child*.

30 C. Clulow in C. Clulow (ed.), *Adult Attachment and Couple Psychotherapy: The 'Secure Base' in Practice and Research* (Brunner-Routledge, 2001), p. 44.

31 Winnicott, *Playing and Reality*, p. 108.

32 Hopper, 'Communication between Mothers and Fetuses'.

33 J. Scharff & D. Scharff, *Object Relations Individual Therapy* (Karnac, 1998).

34 Winnicott, *Playing and Reality*, p. 41.

35 Winnicott ,*The Maturational Processes and the Facilitating Environment*, p. 187.

36 S. Briggs, *Working with Adolescents: a Contemporary Psychodynamic Approach* (Basic Texts in Counselling & Psychotherapy) (Palgrave Macmillan, 2002).

37 Winnicott, *Playing and Reality*, p. 51.

Chapter 5

38 D. Winnicott, *Therapeutic Consultations in Child Psychiatry* (Maresfield Library) (Karnac, 1996).

39 J. Allan, *Inscapes of the Child's World* (Dallas: Spring Publications, 1992).

40 A. Chesner in S. Jennings et al., *The Handbook of Dramatherapy* (Routledge, 1995), p. 116.

41 B. Bettelheim, *The Uses of Enchantment: the Meaning and Importance of Fairy Tales* (Penguin Psychology) (Penguin, 1991).

Chapter 6

42 V. Sinason, 'The psychotherapeutic needs of the learning disabled and multiply disabled child', pp. 445–6 in M. Lanyado & A. Horne (eds), *The Handbook of Child and Adolescent Therapy* (Routledge, 2000), p. 448.

Chapter 7

43 DfES, *The Children Act and Reports 2004* Crown Copyright.

Chapter 8

44 W. Bion, *Clinical Seminars and Other Works* (Karnac, 2000), p. 61.
45 Dockar-Drysdale, *Provision of Primary Experience*, p. 36.
46 M. Klein, *Love, Guilt and Reparation: And Other Works 1921–1945* (Free Press, 2002).
47 W. Fairbairn, *Psychoanalytic Studies of the Personality* (Routledge, 1994).

Chapter 9

48 A. Ward, *Working in Group Care* (Venture Press, 1993).
49 P. Bruggen & C. O'Brian, *Helping Families* (Faber & Faber, 1987).
50 S. Reid, 'The group as a healing whole: group psychotherapy with children and adolescents', pp. 247–59 in M. Lanyado & A. Horne (eds), *The Handbook of Child and Adolescent Psychotherapy* (Routledge, 2000), pp. 257–8.

BIBLIOGRAPHY

J. Allan, *Inscapes of the Child's World* (Spring Publications, 1992)

V. Axline, *Dibs: In Search of Self* (Penguin, 1990)

V. Axline, *Play Therapy* (Ballantine Books, 1981)

A. Bannister *Creative Therapies with Traumatized Children* (Jessica Kingsley, 2003)

BACP, *Ethical Framework for Good Practice in Counselling and Psychotherapy* (BACP, 2002)

B. Bettelheim, *The Uses of Enchantment: the Meaning and Importance of Fairy Tales* (Penguin Psychology) (Penguin, 1991)

B. Bettelheim, *Freud and Man's Soul* (Pimlico, 2001)

B. Bettelheim, *The Informed Heart* (Penguin, 1991)

W. Bion, *Clinical Seminars and Other Works* (Karnac, 2000)

T. Bond, *Standards and Ethics for Counselling in Action* (Counselling in Action Series) (Sage, 2000)

J. Bowlby, *A Secure Base* (Routledge, 1988)

J. Bowlby, *Attachment and Loss: Attachment Vol 1 (Attachment and Loss)* (Pimlico, 1997)

R. Bowlby, *Fifty Years of Attachment Theory: Recollections of Donald Winnicott and John Bowlby* (Karnac, 2004)

B. Brazelton & T. Cramer, *The Earliest Relationship: Parents, Infants and the Drama of Early Attachment* (Karnac, 1991)

S. Briggs, *Working with Adolescents: A Contemporary Psychodynamic Approach* (Basic Texts in Counselling & Psychotherapy) (Palgrave Macmillan, 2002)

P. Bruggen & C. O'Brian, *Helping* Families (Faber & Faber, 1987)

J. Cassidy & P. Shaver (eds) *Handbook of Attachment: Theory, Research and Clinical Applications* (Guilford Press, 2002)

A. Cattanach, *Play Therapy with Abused Children* (Jessica Kingsley, 1992)

A. Chesner in S. Jennings et al., *The Handbook of Dramatherapy* (Routledge, 1995)

P. Clarkson, *The Therapeutic Relationship* (Whurr, 2003)

C. Clulow (ed.), *Adult Attachment and Couple Psychotherapy: "The Secure Base" in Practice and Research* (Brunner-Routledge, 2001)

DfES, *The Children Act and Reports 2004* (DfES, 2004)

B. Dockar-Drysdale, *The Provision of Primary Experience: Winnicottian Work with Children and Adolescents* (Free Association Books, 1990)

B. Dockar-Drysdale, *Therapy and Consultation in Child Care* (Free Association Books, 1993)

E. Erikson, *Identity and the Life Cycle* (W.W. Norton & Co., 1994)

E. Erikson, *Childhood and Society* (Vintage, 1995)

W. Fairbairn, *Psychoanalytic Studies of the Personality* (Routledge, 1994)

C. Feltham (ed.), *Understanding the Counselling Relationship* (Professional Skills for Counsellors Series) (Sage, 1999)

S. Freiberg, *The Magic Years* (Simon & Schuster, 1996)

A. Freud, *The Ego and Mechanisms of Defence* (Karnac, 1993)

S. Freud, *Historical and Expository Works on Psychoanalysis* (Penguin Freud Library) (Penguin, 1993)

L. Gomez, *An Introduction to Object Relations* (Free Association Books, 1997)

L. Gomez, Humanistic or psychodynamic – What is the difference and do we have a choice? *Self & Society* 31(6) (Feb./Mar. 2004)

A. Gray, *An Introduction to the Psychotherapeutic Frame* (Routledge, 1994)

J. Harris-Hendriks et al., *When Father Kills Mother* (Routledge, 2000)

M. Herbert, *Working with Children and the Children Act* (BPS Books 1996)

D. Hindle & M. Smith (eds), *Personality Development: A Psychoanalytic Perspective* (Routledge, 1999)

J. Holmes, *John Bowlby and Attachment Theory* (Makers of Modern Psychotherapy Series) (Routledge, 1993)

L. Hopper, Communication between Mothers and Fetuses (thesis, University of Reading, 1993)

M. Hunter, *Psychotherapy with Young People in Care: Lost and Found* (Brunner-Routledge, 2001)

M. Jacobs, *D.W. Winnicott* (Key Figures in Counselling Series) (Sage, 1993)

M. Jacobs, *The Presenting Past: An introduction to Practical Psychodynamic Counselling* (Open University Press, 1992)

M. Jacobs, *Psychodynamic Counselling in Action* (Counselling in Action Series) (Sage, 2004)

P. Jenkins, *Counselling, Psychotherapy and the Law* (Professional Skills for Counsellors Series) (Sage, 1999)

D. Judd, *Give Sorrow Words* (Whurr, 1995)

M. Klein, *Love, Guilt and Reparation: And Other Works 1921–1945* (Free Press, 2002)

M. Klein, *Psychoanalysis of Children* (Contemporary Classics Series) (Vintage, 1997)

M. Lanyado, *The Presence of the Therapist: Treating Childhood Trauma* (Brunner-Routledge, 2004)

A. Lester, *The Angry Christian A Theology for Care and Counselling* (Westminster John Knox Press, 2003)

M. Mahler et al., *The Psychological Birth of the Human Infant* : Symbiosis and Individuation (Karnac Classics) (Karnac, 2002)

L. McMahon, *The Handbook of Play Therapy* (Routledge, 1992)

S. Palmer et al., *Ethical Framework for Good Practice in Counselling and Psychotherapy* (BACP, 2002)

N. Parker, Eating disorders. In M. Lanyado & A. Horne (eds), *The Handbook of Child and Adolescent Psychotherapy* (Routledge, 2000), pp. 387–404.

A. Piontelli, *From Fetus to Child: an Observational and Psychoanalytic Study* (New Library of Psychoanalysis) (Routledge, 1992)

M. Rustin & E. Quagliata (eds), *Assessment in Child Psychotherapy* (Tavistock Clinic Series) (Duckworth, 2000)

S. Reid, The group as a healing whole: Group psychotherapy with children and adolescents. In M. Lanyado & A. Horne (eds), *The Handbook of Child and Adolescent Psychotherapy* (Routledge, 2000), pp. 247–59.

Samaritans, the, *Key Facts: Young People and Suicide* (Ewell: The Samaritans, 2001)

A. Sansone, *Mothers, Babies and Their Body Language* (Karnac, 2004)

J. Scharff & D. Scharff, *Object Relations Individual Therapy* (Karnac, 1998)

J. Segal, *Melanie Klein* (Key Figures in Counselling Series) (Sage, 2004)

V. Sinason, The psychotherapeutic needs of the learning disabled and multiply disabled child. In M. Lanyado & A. Horne (eds), *The Handbook of Child and Adolescent Psychotherapy* (Routledge, 2000), pp. 445–56

L. Spurling, *An Introduction to Psychodynamic Counselling* (Basic Texts in Counselling & Psychotherapy) (Palgrave Macmillan, 2004)

D. Stern, *The First Relationship: Infant and Mother* (Harvard University Press, 2004)

D. Stern, *The Interpersonal World of the Infant: A View from Psychoanalysis and Development Psychology* (Karnac, 1998)

D. Stern, *The First Relationship: Infant and Mother* (Harvard University Press, 2004)

F. Tustin, *The Protective Shell in Children and Adults* (Karnac, 1990)

T. Verny & J. Kelly, *The Secret Life of the Unborn Child* (Times Warner Paperbacks, 1988)

A. Ward, *Working in Group Care* (Venture Press, 1993)

O. Weininger, *View from the Cradle: Children's Emotions in Everyday Life* (Karnac, 1993)

D. Winnicott, *Babies and Their Mothers* (Free Association Books, 1988)

D. Winnicott, *Home is Where We Start From: Essays by a Psychoanalyst* (Penguin, 1990)

D. Winnicott, *Playing and Reality* (Routledge Classics) (Routledge, 2005)

D. Winnicott, *The Child, the Family and the Outside World* (Penguin, 1991)

D. Winnicott, *The Family and Individual Development* (Routledge, 1968)

D. Winnicott *The Maturational Processes and the Facilitating Environment* (Maresfield Library) (Karnac, 1990)

D. Winnicott, *The Piggle: An Account of the Psychoanalytic Treatment of a Little Girl* (Penguin Psychology) (Penguin, 1991)

D. Winnicott, *Therapeutic Consultations in Child Psychiatry* (Maresfield Library) (Karnac, 1996)

D. Winnicott, *Thinking about Children* (Karnac, 1996)

D Winnicott, *Through Paediatrics to Psychoanalysis: Collected Papers* (Brunner-Routledge, 1992)

INDEX